LOG

MW00788347

Contemporary Logo Design

GINGKO PRESS

LOGOISM

Contemporary Logo Design

ISBN 978-1-58423-654-2

First Published in the United States of America by
Gingko Press by arrangement with
Sandu Publishing Co., Ltd.

Gingko Press, Inc.
1321 Fifth Street
Berkeley, CA 94710 USA
Tel: (510) 898 1195
Fax: (510) 898 1196
Email: books@gingkopress.com
www.gingkopress.com

Copyright © 2017 by Sandu Publishing
First published in 2017 by Sandu Publishing

Sponsored by Design 360°
– Concept and Design Magazine

Edited and produced by
Sandu Publishing Co., Ltd.

Book design, concepts & art direction by
Sandu Publishing Co., Ltd.
Chief Editor: Wang Shaoqiang
Design Director: Niu Huizhen

info@sandupublishing.com
www.sandupublishing.com

Printed and bound in China

CONTENTS

PREFACE _____ 006

SYMBOL _____ 009

TYPE _____ 057

SYMBOL & TYPE _____ 121

FORM _____ 185

ENSEMBLE _____ 233

RETRO _____ 281

INDEX _____ 314

ACKNOWLEDGEMENTS _____ 320

PREFACE

*by **Maurizio Pagnozzi***

The brand mark, or logo, is a set of graphic and typographic symbols that identify a company or a product in order to differentiate it from its competitors — an important consideration, especially today when the modern consumer has a myriad of products to choose from.

The first step before becoming immersed in the creative design process is to understand what the roles of a logo are. There are three fundamental roles that designers must always consider before creating a logo:

1) the identification role: a customer must be able to distinguish a company or a product in the market by the logo. The logo, therefore, must be identifiable and recognizable.

2) the distinction role: a successful logo must be unique and original, must differentiate a company from its competitors and offer something extra that attracts the customer to it.

3) the communication role: a logo should be able to communicate a message. A poorly designed logo could convey a wrong, unprofessional, misleading or outdated message.

The task of a good designer is to determine how to express these concepts visually as well as create the logo's style. It is also essential to remember that all of the elements used in designing a logo should reflect the values previously established for that brand. This goal can be achieved through the use of carefully considered colors and forms. For example, if the goal of a specific company is to communicate a clear sense of "elegance" or "fun", the shapes, the colors and the lettering of the logo must help to convey that message.

But even before applying colors and lettering, we must make sure the style used is consistent with the target, and that the symbolic "code" of the logo is understandable to the audience. If we use an incomprehensible symbol to communicate with the audience, even if the logo seems perfect, it will be difficult to understand and thus will not work. This code must also allow an informal understanding across various platforms, eliminating the "loss in translation" that is possible when the logo is used in different applications. It is essential to use the right code in logo design, as it will ultimately be linked to the visual perception process. The correct code will allow an international logo to be understood even in different countries, beyond the language used in that particular country.

Since beginning my career as a designer I have mainly focused on branding and logo design. Very often people ask me what the secret to creating a good logo is. Honestly, when I start designing a logo, I focus on two main goals: to make an enduring modern logo, and to keep it in contact with the target audience.

Generally, a company tends to maintain the logo that has made it famous as an element of strength, consistency and visibility to the public. A logo is not like a brochure or a flyer that is temporary, used only for a few weeks or months. A logo will last for years until the next redesign. The biggest challenge is to make it contemporary for years to come. But what makes a contemporary logo? In today's digital world, we are always on the go — we need intuitive things that support us no matter where we are located, or what time it is. So a modern logo must also be intuitive and dynamic, flexible and adaptable.

The second aspect that I work with is contact with the public as an audience. A logo represents the first essential element of a visual identity: to support the mission of a company. The mission is the ultimate purpose of the enterprise, the reason for its existence, and the meaning for its presence in the market; it is also something distinctive, an element that differentiates it from competitors. Analysis of a brand must first focus on the elements that really matter; often it happens that the brand designer takes into account too many elements, losing sight of the distinctive features of a product, service or company. This can eventually damage communication with their audience.

An effective logo is distinctive, appropriate, practical, graphically engaging, simple in form and able to convey an intended message. In its simplest form, a logo is there to identify, but to do this effectively it must follow the basic principles of logo design. Overall, a logo must be simple. A simple logo allows for easy recognition and allows the logo to be versatile and memorable. Effective logos feature something unexpected or unique without being overdrawn.

Following closely behind the principle of simplicity is that of memorability. An effective logo will achieve this by having a simple yet appropriate design.

Other factors a logo must speak to include:

— A logo must be enduring; it should be able to withstand the test of time. The logo should be "future proof", meaning that it should still be effective in ten or twenty more years.

— A logo must be versatile. A design should be able to work across a variety of mediums and applications, with the ability to be used in digital representations.

— A logo must be appropriate. The design and positioning of the logo should be appropriate for its intended purpose.

In the following pages we will see how designers from around the world have tried to express these ideals in visual logo design for numerous brands. A selection of different logos are classified into 6 groups — symbol, type, symbol and type, form, ensemble, and retro. This book will inspire and motivate you to make smart and well-informed decisions when procuring and working with your own clients.

Maurizio Pagnozzi
One Design

www.mauriziopagnozzi.com

Maurizio Pagnozzi is an Italian designer based in London, specialized in branding, corporate identity, and packaging. He studied graphic design at "Scuola la Tecnica of Benevento," where he graduated with a project entitled "Anatomy of the typeface." He continued his studies at ILAS of Naples, where he studied art direction and copywriting and where he attended a master program in graphic design. He graduated in 2013 with full marks honors. He carries out freelance activities at his studio, One Design. He has worked for several international clients who appreciate his design style, which is clean and direct but not devoid of meaning and content. His aim is to create works that combine concepts with strong function and solid execution.

SYMBOL

In the world of modern logo design, "less is more" has gradually become a popular trend. Following the principle of simplicity, more and more designers tend to use minimal elements to reflect the essence of their client company. Without complicated details, these emblematic designs capture attention and communicate a variety of information.

The Interview with
PISTINEGA

*by **Maurizio Pagnozzi***

1. As a graphic designer, where do you typically look for design inspiration?

I am inspired by daily life; I was always a strong observer. Wherever I am, I look around myself to try to see something that can catch my attention; if something causes emotion, it is probably a great source of inspiration, therefore I take a picture and keep it in my hard drive to pull it out at the right time. Occasionally I take inspiration from nature, sometimes also from the urban environment. Even a modern art museum can be an excellent source of inspiration! The secret is to be curious — this is the reason why I recommend you to listen music, watch videos, read books, analyze articles, and look constantly for new things. During the creative process, these suggestions may become very useful.

Finally, a thought regarding the inspiration that comes from books of design. I know that a piece of paper does not seem enchanting, but if you need ideas or a guide to help create, or get over a creative block, magazines and specialized books can be a great help. I often feel that looking through a book is more useful and relaxing than watching something on a screen.

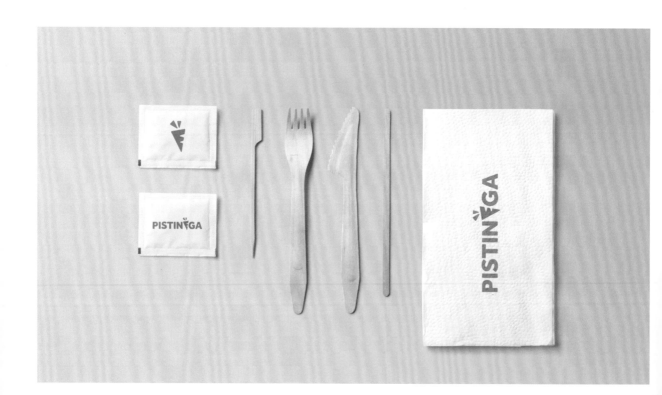

2. What is your typical design process when designing a logo for a new client?

My creative process to find the right idea is divided into the analysis of the brief, the brainstorm, and the conceptual maps. I start inspiring and sketching new ideas, testing the strongest, and trying to be as original as possible. I try to improve and develop the sketches to bring them to a higher level, then I draw the logo again, paying careful attention to the thickness and construction of lines. I import the draft in Illustrator, where I define the typography, kerning, lettering layout, proportions, and colors. I Google it to verify if other designers have already created something similar to my new project. Finally I choose the best creation, and before sending it to the client I make a final review — for example, checking if anything can be visually improved. I also attach an explanation of the concept and the creative process followed, as well as a series of mockups that simulate how the logo will appear on several digital and/or non-digital supports.

3. What images did you have in mind while you were designing the logo for the juice bar "Pistinèga"?

The "Pistinèga" project is for a juice bar in Bologna, Italy, and I think the cool thing about the end result is how clever the solution was for the logo. The name of the juice bar is Pistinèga, which means "carrot" in the Bolognese dialect. I simply played with negative space to create the letter E from the shadows in a carrot.

The logo concept below demonstrates how the thoughtful combination of the letter, carrot and drink forms clean, crisp logo. The strict use of shape and color keeps the branding consistent. As a juicing company, the variety of products sold (including snacks) made for a range of brand materials not typically associated with a juice brand. I kept this in mind when I drew it and I have tried to translate this concept into the shape.

4. What feeling or message do you want the logo "Pistinèga" to convey to those who view it?

The name of the bar is the starting point that I used to develop the concept. The Pistinèga logo merges the "È" of Pistinèga, the carrot and the juice drink to refer to the most representative aspects of what the bar serves.

During the briefing, the client and I decided on an image that would express a sense of freshness, greenery, nature and life, but also quality and health, all in a contemporary and captivating style that would lend itself well across the entire brand image. The carrot is used in the lettering of Pistinèga, but can also be used alone as an icon while still maintaining brand recognition.

The final logo works both on its own and repeated as a pattern, as well as when integrated into the name of the establishment.

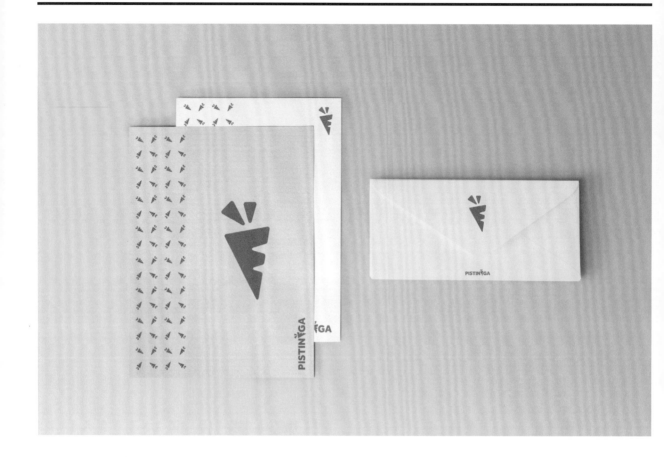

5. In your opinion, what makes a good logo?

There are some key aspects that make great a logo — for example, the minimalism, the readability, the recognition, the memorability, and the uniqueness. In addition, there are two other important features that should be considered during the creation of a new logo: its durability and its versatility over several physical or digital media. A good logo doesn't go out of fashion and has good versatility.

6. Your top three pieces of advice for logo/brand identity design beginners?

Having a look at the projects of specialists to identify how they express these characteristics might be a good exercise for those approaching logo design for the first time. And again, keep up to date; know what the trends are in the field. Healthy curiosity supported by study is a key to success in the field. And finally, find your own recognizable style, and always be unique and original.

1. GoAnimate

Design: Alexander Tsanev
Client: GoAnimate

2. Odola Technologies

Design: Andrea Pinter

3. Tempco 2nd Approach

Design: Misael Osorio
Client: Tempco Air Supply

4. CEN

Design: Misael Osorio
Client: CEN

5. Maquinados

Design: Misael Osorio
Client: Maquinados de
Automatización Avanzada

6. Tempco 1st Approach

Design: Misael Osorio
Client: Tempco Air Supply

1

2

3

4

5

6

7. Sky Sports

Design: Alexander Morgan
Client: Sky Sports

8. Proverni

Design: Abstract Logic
Client: Ivan Klimov

9. Alexander Morgan

Design: Alexander Morgan
Client: Alexander Morgan

10. Y Mark

Design: Alexander Morgan
Client: Yasari Yaj

11. Prime Visa

Design: Abstract Logic
Client: Prime Visa

12. Digital Artwerks

Design: Stefan Grubačić
Client: Digital Artwerks Media

7

8

9

10

11

12

1. MA

Design: Andrea Schlaffer
Client: Molnar Anna

2. NORRTE

Design: DUNA
Client: Norrte Engenharia

3. Transforma

Design: Misael Osorio
Client: Transforma

4. ORS

Design: Misael Osorio
Client: Office of Resilience
and Sustainability –
El Paso Tx.

5. Público General

Design: Misael Osorio
Client: Público General

6. Delgado Aberturas

Design: Morocho Estudio
Client: Delgado Aberturas

1

2

3

4

5

6

7. Nonet

Design: Misael Osorio
Client: Nonet

8. BookitZone

Design: Denys Kotliarov
Client: BookitZone Ltd.

9. Nen's

Design: Misael Osorio
Client: Nen's

10. U11

Design: Alexander Tsanev
Client: Hype Digital Agency

11. Casa Cárnica — **Frutas**

Design: Misael Osorio
Client: Casa Cárnica

7

8

9

10

11

1. Yellowbear

Design: Zivan Rosic
Client: Yellowbear Financial Consultancy

2. Jagged

Design: Dušan Miletć
Client: Jagged

3. Overlap C Studios

Design: Dušan Miletć
Client: Overlap C

4. Fast Bus

Design: Alaa Tameem
Client: Public transportation

5. Ecopure

Design: monome
Client: ecopure

6. Bellomed

Design: Dušan Miletć
Client: Bellomed

1

2

3

4

5

6

7

8

9

10

11

12

7. Linbird

Design: monome
Client: linbird

8. Dronone

Design: monome
Client: dronone

9. Fragrance Oils

Design: Denys Kotliarov
Client: Fragrance Oils

10. Kulturhavn

Design: Zivan Rosic
Client: Kulturhavn Festival

11. Passenger 7

Design: Zivan Rosic
Client: Passenger 7

12. Slate Building Group

Design: Dušan Miletć
Client: Slate Building Group

1. Easter Egg hunt

Design: Alexander Tsanev
Client: DirektHolidays

2. Penguins Ski School

Design: Alexander Tsanev
Client: DirektHolidays

3. Bisantz Beekeepers

Design: Alexander Tsanev
Client: Sonja Bizantz

4. The Owls

Design: Alexander Tsanev
Client: The Owls

5. Firefox

Design: Alexander Morgan
Client: Firefox

6. Casa Cárnica – Pollo

Design: Misael Osorio
Client: Casa Cárnica

1

2

3

4

5

6

7. Happy Whale

Design: Andrea Pinter

8. BKP Law Office

Design: Fuzz Studio
Client: Blasza
Krol i Partnerzy

9. Made in mozg

Design: Denys Kotliarov
Client: Made in mozg

10. Golden Retriever

Design: Daniel Owen Comite
Client: Self Promotion

11. PetShop

Design: FLAT12 studio
Client: PetShop

12. Quadro Soft

Design: Denys Kotliarov
Client: Quadro Soft

7

8

9

10

11

12

1. Era3

Design: Denys Kotliarov
Client: Era3

2. F – cosmetic institute

Design: POSITIVE designlab
Client: Artemis Eleftheriadou

3. NO HALFTIME

Design: Oscar Bastidas
Client: No Halftime —
Fantasy Sport APP

4. Eco Drop

Design: Daniel Owen Comite
Client: Eco Drop

**5. Sustainable
Harvesting Pledge**

Design: Daniel Owen Comite
Client: US Sustainable
Harvesters Asc.

6. CCI Guide Dogs

Design: Daniel Owen Comite
Client: Canine Companions
for Independence

1

2

3

4

5

6

7. Moskio

Design: Inluw Team
Client: Moskio

8. Migrant Heritage

Design: Alexander Tsanev
Client: Bulgarian
Academy of Sciences

9. TAIKIN

Design: Oscar Bastidas
Client: Taikin Asian Cuisine –
Asian Restaurant in Florida

10. Raspberry's Veranda

Design: Fuzz Studio
Client: Invitro

11. Surf Sushi

Design: Daniel Owen Comite
Client: Surf Sushi

12. Star Shaker

Design: Abstract Logic
Client: Star Shaker

7

8

9

10

11

12

1. Tek Talent

Design: Angelos Botsis
Client: Tektalent Ltd.

2. Herimeheri

Design: Angelos Botsis
Client: Herimeheri. Extra
Virgin Olive oil Products

3. Fly Addiction

Design: Botond Vörös
Client: Fly Addiction

4. Subjective Contour

Design: Botond Vörös
Client: MATT

5. Open Day

Design: Botond Vörös
Client: Hungarian University
of Fine Arts

6. Klear

Design: Asen Petrov
Client: Klear Lending

1

2

3

4

5

6

7

8

7. Chinof

Design: Asen Petrov
Client: Stefan Chinof

8. MODO

Design: Asen Petrov
Client: Modo —
The Jewellery Studio

9. Starck Architecture and Planning

Design: Asen Petrov
Client: Starck Architecture
and Planning

10. Hadjivanov

Design: Asen Petrov
Client: Light
Capture Photography

11. Cocoon Health Group

Design: StudioMH
Client: Cocoon Health Group

12. Ward and Condrey

Design: Odie+Partners
Client: Ward and Condrey

9

10

11

12

1. Surepoint

Design: Kimmy Lee
Client: Self-initiated Project

2. Leaf

Design: Kimmy Lee
Client: Self-initiated Project

3. Logo

Design: Maurizio Pagnozzi
Client: Maurizio Pagnozzi

4. Basegrill

Design: Chris Trivizas
Client: Basegrill

5. Voodoo Tattoo

Design: Alexander Morgan
Client: Voodoo

1

2

3

4

5

6. AMA

Design: Henríquez
Lara Estudio
Client: AMA

7. E-Cart

Design: Kimmy Lee
Client: Self-initiated Project

8. Eye

Design: Andrea Schlaffer
Client: Eye Inc.

9. Flower Patch

Design: Kimmy Lee
Client: Self-initiated Project

10. Moresca XV

Design: Henríquez
Lara Estudio
Client: La Moresca

11. Flōs – Letterbox Flowers

Design: Giada Tamborrino
Client: Personal Project

6

7

8

9

10

11

1. Cassie Condrey

Design: Odie+Partners
Client: Cassie Condrey

**2. Marta – Women
Urban Clothing**

Design: Dawid Cmok

3. Virago

Design: Anna Kuts
Client: Virago

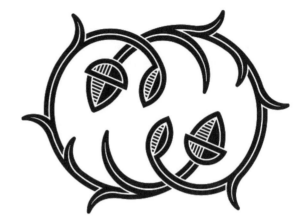

1

2

3

4

4. Machuastik

Design: Mostasho
Client: Daniel Uribe

5. Oxlot 9

Design: Odie+Partners
Client: Oxlot 9

6. Canopy Construction

Design: Odie+Partners
Client: Canopy Construction

5

6

1. Artum

Design: Dave Klimek
Client: Artum

2. Property Force

Design: Anna Kuts
Client: Property Force

3. Merqio

Design: Dave Klimek
Client: Merqio

4. TechFides Solutions

Design: Dave Klimek
Client: TechFides

5. Argus

Design: Dave Klimek
Client: Argus

6. Nagy

Design: Dave Klimek
Client: Nagy

1

2

3

4

5

6

7

8

9

10

11

12

7. Beltissimo

Design: Dave Klimek
Client: Beltissimo

8. Tesla Medical

Design: Dave Klimek
Client: Tesla Medical

9. Oaks Lab

Design: Dave Klimek
Client: Oaks Lab

10. Garici

Design: Dave Klimek
Client: Garici

11. Profi Parfums

Design: Dave Klimek
Client: Profi Parfums

12. Fortis

Design: Anna Kuts
Client: Fortis

1. Electrowave

Design: Daria Stetsenko
Client: Electrowave

2. WOK & LOVE

Design: Angelos Botsis
Client: Wok & Love

3. RFFY

Design: Panfilov & Yushko
Creative Group
Client: RFFY

1   2

3

4. Selectiv

Design: Zivan Rosic
Client: Selectiv

5. Nelson Design

Design: Two Times Elliott
Client: Nelson Design

6. Film Poets

Design: Odie+Partners
Client: Film Poets

7. Odme

Design: Two Times Elliott
Client: Odme

8. Kanica Weaving

Design: Angelos Botsis
Client: Laura Vargas Llianas

9. Lagora Pools

Design: Odie+Partners
Client: Lagora Pools

4

5

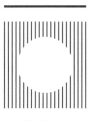

6

7

8

9

1. Ekoterinburg

Design: Typemate
Client: Public ecological
movement in Ekaterinburg

2. Your Own

Shoes Company

Design: Typemate
Client: Your Own Shoes
Company / Logomachine

3. YOURDRS

Design: Anna Kuts
Client: Yourdrs

4. El Patio

Design: Misael Osorio
Client: El Patio

5. One Two Team

Design: Anna Kuts
Client: One Two Team

6. Casa Clementina

Design: Henríquez
Lara Estudio
Client: Casa Clementina

1

2

3

4

5

6

7

8

9

10

11

12

7. Castles of Ukraine
Design: Daria Stetsenko
Client: KSADA

8. PineDev Studio
Design: Daria Stetsenko
Client: PineDev Studio

9. Lover Blazer
Design: Giada Tamborrino
Client: The Lover Blazer
– Fashion Blog

10. Sushi
Design: Kimmy Lee
Client: Self-initiated Project

11. Rhodehouse Realestate
Design: Vlad Penev
Client: Rhodehouse Real
Estate LLC

12. Sergey Zhmykov
Design: Daria Stetsenko
Client: Sergey Zhmykov

1. Bent Taco

Design: vacaliebres
Client: Bent Taco

2. Typefind

Design: Sean O'Connor
Client: Typefind

3. Peacemakers team

Design: Typemate
Client: Extreme sports wear

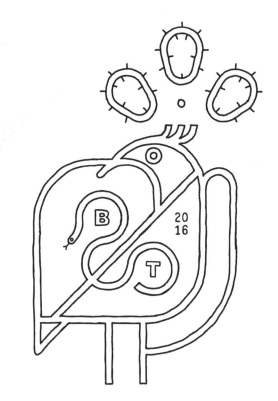

1

2

3

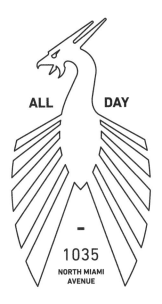

4

4. ALL DAY MIAMI

Design: vacaliebres
Client: ALL DAY MIAMI

5. White Owl Pin

Design: vacaliebres
Client: vacaliebres

5

1. IV

Design: Value Studio
Client: Vladimir Ilnitskiy

2. Team UP

Design: Odie+Partners
Client: Team UP

3. LineWorks Engineering

Design: Odie+Partners
Client: LineWorks
Engineering

4. EQ

Design: sstudio™
Client: Espacio Quiñihual

5. Castles of Ukraine

Design: Daria Stetsenko
Client: KSADA

6. Dick Clark

Design: Odie+Partners
Client: Dick Clark

1

2

3

4

5

6

7

8

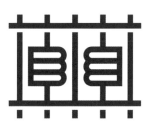

9

10

11

12

7. DBDI

Design: Nick Zotov
Client: DBDI

8. TD

Design: sstudio™
Client: TD

9. Tashkeel Studio

Design: Alaa Tameem
Client: Tashkeel

10. Bail Bond Brothers

Design: Odie+Partners
Client: Bail Bond Brothers

11. Robotic Solutions

Design: Nick Zotov
Client: Safety
Robotic Solutions

12. Millers Motorcycle

Design: Nick Zotov
Client: Millers Motors

1. Interlock eSports

Design: Five Designs™
Client: Interlock eSports

2. Alset

Design: Henríquez
Lara Estudio
Client: Alset

3. McDonald & Butler

Design: Kevin
Harald Campean
Client: McDonald & Butler

4. Alvicom

Design: Kevin
Harald Campean
Client: Alvicom

5. MPower

Design: Pavel Saksin
Client: MPower
Property Solutions

6. Asen Petrov

Design: Asen Petrov
Client: Personal Mark

1

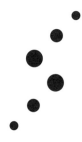

2

3

4

5

6

7. Top Coat

Design: Odie+Partners
Client: Top Coat

8. Little Drop

Design: Anna Kuts
Client: Bigdrop

9. THOR

Design: Stefan Grubačić
Client: THOR Trucks

10. Anyone

Design: Dawid Cmok
Client: Anyone

11. FNBLINK

Design: Anna Kuts
Client: FNBLINK

12. Worksquarz

Design: Anna Kuts
Client: Worksquarz

7

8

9

10

11

12

1. Nezeritis

Design: Luminous
Design Group
Client: Nezeritis Photography

2. RF – DJ

Design: Stefan Grubačić
Client: RF – DJ

3. TT / Talkin' Threads

Design: Maurizio Pagnozzi
Client: Talkin' Threads

4. Eastern Synergy

Design: Alaa Tameem
Client: Eastern
Synergy Contracting

5. Tanya Bulgakova

Design: Anna Kuts
Client: Tanya Bulgakova

6. Borisov Photography

Design: Vlad Penev
Client: Mr. Borisov

1

2

3

4

5

6

7. Reelevant

Design: Pavel Saksin
Client: Reelevant

8. Katerina Zamoriy

Design: Anna Kuts
Client: Katerina Zamoriy

9. King elephant

Design: Pavel Saksin
Client: King elephant

10. Squid

Design: Kimmy Lee
Client: Self-initiated Project

11. LVC

Design: Stefan Grubačić
Client: LVC Winery

7

8

9

10

11

1. El Rey

Design: Misael Osorio
Client: El Rey

2. Wedding of Architects

Design: Anna Kuts
Client: Denis & Julia Shataliuk

3. Indian Gardens

Design: Nebojsa Matkovic
Client: Indian Gardens

4. Jo

Design: Angelos Botsis
Client: Jo Coiffure

5. Jade Riccio – Soprano

Design: Kimmy Lee
Client: Self-initiated Project

6. Tea for Tango

Design: Milos Milovanovic
Client: Florentina
Flor Salvador

1

2

3

4

5

1. NIKE DIGITAL VANDALS

Design: OSOM STUDIOS

2. OSOM STUDIOS

Design: OSOM STUDIOS
Client: OSOM STUDIOS

3. Prague Cargo Bike

Design: Dave Klimek
Client: Prague Cargo Bike

4. Ubirouting

Design: Pavel Saksin
Client: Ubirouting

5. William Gray

Design: Odie+Partners
Client: William Gray

1

2

3

4

5

6

7

8

9

10

11

6. Cos

Design: Henríquez
Lara Estudio
Client: Cos

**7. Consumerism is the
new Religion**

Design: Giada Tamborrino
Client: Exhibition
about "Consumerism"

8. Centaur

Design: Nick Zotov
Client: Centaur Inc.

9. TAURUS

Design: Matthieu Martigny
Client: Self-initiated Project

10. Matthias Kaupermann

Design: Odie+Partners
Client: Matthias Kaupermann

11. DNLS Monogram

Design: Mostasho
Agency: Skinpop Studio
Client: Los Daniels

1. David Mathews Center

Design: Odie+Partners
Client: David Mathews Center

2. Heron

Design: Margarita Petrianova
Client: Valeria Petrianova

3. Open Thessaloniki

Design: Angelos Botsis
Client: Open Thessaloniki

4. Coffeemore

Design: Mostasho
Agency: Skinpop Studio
Client: Coffeemore –
Yogurt & Coffee

5. Rainbow Warefare

Design: Mostasho
Agency: Skinpop Studio
Client: John Ferraris

6. Mostasho

Design: Mostasho
Client: Mostasho

1

2

3

4

5

6

7

8

7. Simply

Design: Pavel Saksin
Client: Simply

8. Steven Tabach

Design: Anna Kuts
Client: Steven Tabach

9. Before box office

Design: Pavel Saksin
Client: Before box office

10. Perros de la calle

Design: sstudio™
Client: Perros de la Calle

11. PICTURAL LINE

Design: Matthieu Martigny
Client: Self-initiated Project

12. Mason Music

Design: Odie+Partners
Client: Mason Music

9

10

11

12

1. Track 1

Design: KR8 bureau

2. 4

Design: sstudio™
Client: 4

3. 55 Max

Design: Two Times Elliott
Client: 55 Max

4. 55 Max

Design: Two Times Elliott
Client: 55 Max

5. 7 Hair

Design: Asen Petrov
Client: 7 Hair

6. 99 INFINITY

Design: Matthieu Martigny
Client: Self-initiated Project

1

2

3

4

5

6

7

8

7. a Mark

Design: Asen Petrov

8. Achilles

Design: Botond Vörös
Client: Hungarian
University of Fine Arts

9. Adtention

Design: Nick Zotov
Client: Adtention

10. A Design

Design: Matthieu Martigny
Client: Self-initiated Project

11. Bike Story

Design: Maciej Świerczek
Client: Bike Story

12. Bohema

Design: Konrad Sybilski
Client: Bohema Clothing

9

10

11

12

1. Bondster

Design: Dave Klimek
Client: Bondster

2. B Music

Design: Alaa Tameem
Client: B Music

3. B LINE

Design: Matthieu Martigny
Client: Self-initiated Project

4. B

Design: Matthieu Martigny
Client: Self-initiated Project

5. Cord

Design: Two Times Elliott
Client: Cord

6. Slovacke Theater

Design: Dave Klimek
Client: Slovacke Theater

1

2

3

4

5

6

7. TIGER D

Design: Matthieu Martigny
Client: Self-initiated Project

8. Dan Digangi

Design: StudioMH
Client: Dan Digangi

9. Studio Dunn

Design: Two Times Elliott
Client: Studio Dunn

10. Estheutical

Design: Dave Klimek
Client: Estheutical

11. EastWest Architecture

Design: Two Times Elliott
Client: EastWest Architecture

12. Feeld

Design: Two Times Elliott
Client: Feeld

7

8

9

10

11

12

1. Christopher Hall

Design: Two Times Elliott
Client: Christopher Hall

2. Monique

Design: Noeeko Studio
Client: Monique

**3. Hungarian
Seasoning Paprika**

Design: Botond Vörös
Client: Hungarian University
of Fine Arts

4. Regstav

Design: Nick Zotov
Client: Regstav

5. R

Design: Matthieu Martigny
Client: Self-initiated Project

6. R

Design: Matthieu Martigny
Client: Self-initiated Project

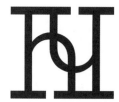

1

2

3

4

5

6

7. S.B. Monogram

Design: Kimmy Lee
Client: Self-initiated Project

8. DOUBLE SS

Design: Matthieu Martigny
Client: Self-initiated Project

9. S.S Monogram

Design: Kimmy Lee
Client: Self-initiated Project

10. Salam Furniture

Design: Alaa Tameem
Client: Saban Classic
Furniture Store

11. Top Efekt

Design: Dave Klimek
Client: Top Efekt

12. Fathom

Design: Two Times Elliott
Client: Fathom

7

8

ETS 1975

9

10

11

12

1. X Comunicar Design

Design: Filipe Guimarães
Client: ESAD.CR

2. Zero Parallel

Design: Anna Kuts
Client: Zero Parallel

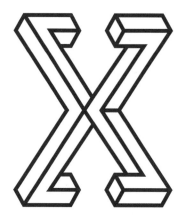

1

2

TYPE

As we all know, type-only logos are some of the most common logo designs, and a creative movement is currently rising in contemporary type design. In the following chapter, you'll discover striking examples that explore the endless graphic possibilities of type. Here, designers strive to break the limits of conventional typography and develop pioneering styles where fonts are slashed, fuzzed, twisted, and more.

The Interview with
Esquina do Avesso

by Another Collective

1. What information do you gather from a client before designing a logo usually?

The information we have depends on the client — there are cases where they give us a very complete briefing and others where they just explain their main goal or desire. But we already have a couple of questions that we always ask in order to fully understand what the project needs.

We feel that we need to be very aware of the concept and to be able to discuss with the client what the strong and weak points of his business are, to get the best solutions. We also request a few examples of what the client expects and appreciates such as colors, typography or other graphic aspects.

2. Where did you find inspiration for the logo "Esquina do Avesso"?

Esquina do Avesso's visual identity is inspired by its location since it is located in a corner. The space's atmosphere is a mix of rustic with modern touches, so we tried to reflect this in the logo by using varied typography. Their menu changes every three months and carries the motto "upside down", which is also the origin of their name. The aesthetics and preferences of the client were also very important to the proposal.

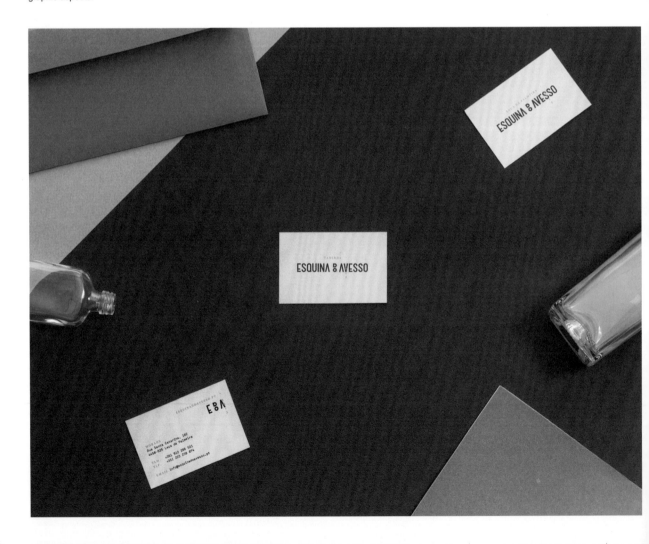

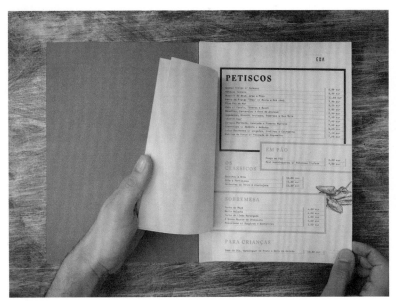

3. Could you please describe the process of designing the logo "Esquina do Avesso"?

Esquina do Avesso was a little bit different from what we were used to doing. In this case, the business's name was also changing, so we had the opportunity to be involved in the naming process.

We also really felt the freedom to explore on this project, and to try several new things with no restrictions in terms of the identity. It was a very interesting creative engagement. The identity was inspired by the architecture and location, and we tried to suggest this in the logo through descriptive type orientation. We also tried to reflect the restaurant's atmosphere in the logo with the color choices, typography, and other aspects.

4. If you could sum up your design philosophy, what would it be?

We don't have a philosophy right now, we are still searching for it. Instead, we have some main principles of how to behave in the creative process. For example, our obligations as designers who live essentially from commercial projects, our behavior in the design field, the relation between the client and the studio, and how we can add to the design in each project. But in our opinion, they are quite far from being our own philosophies.

5. What do you see as the difference between logo design and other graphic design disciplines?

We are not sure if there are differences. In our experience, the qualities needed to develop a project are almost the same for people who make branding as the people who develop editorial design or infographics.

6. In your opinion, what are the most important aspects of designing a logo?

To know the project you are working on. If we don't fully understand the project, the client or the target, the project will be empty, from the finished product to the concept to even the creative work.

1. Ptashka

Design: Inluw Team
Client: Ptashka

2. Chemlit

Design: Inluw Team
Client: Chemlit

3. Supafresh

Design: Inluw Team
Client: Jungle

4. Hipstapatch

Design: Jimbo Bernaus
Client: Hipstapatch

1

2

3

4

5. Fresh Green

Design: Typemate
Client: healthy nutrition bar

6. Grandma's garden

Design: Typemate
Client: Flower delivery

7. Woodstamp

Design: Roman Dzivulskiy
Client: Bird of Happiness

8. Alice Fox

Design: Typemate
Client: handmade souvenirs
in Saint-Petersburg

5

6

7

8

1. Oleshky

Design: Roman Dzivulskiy

2. Anna Mantissa

Design: Value Studio
Client: Anna Mantissa

3. Das Burgeramt

Design: Jimbo Bernaus
Client: Anna Mantissa

4. Mudita

Design: Jimbo Bernaus
Client: Mudita

ОЛЕШКИ

THE CITY OF THE SUN

Anna Mantissa

1

2

Das Burgeramt

3

4

5

6

5. Creature Lab

Design: Jimbo Bernaus
Client: Creature Lab

6. Longinus

Design: Jimbo Bernaus
Client: Longinus

7. Dan Bean

Design: Jimbo Bernaus
Client: Dan Bean

8. Heartbeat

Design: Jimbo Bernaus
Client: Heartbeat
Design Agency

7

8

1. Brasl

Design: Abstract Logic
Client: Brasl

2. Zarechniy

Design: Roman Dzivulskiy
Client: Zarechniy

3. Quick Nails Bar

Design: Fuzz Studio
Client: Quick Nails Bar

4. Woogies

Design: Studio AIO
Client: Woogies

5. Sem' dorog

Design: Roman Dzivulskiy
Client: Sem' dorog

6. Fanny Finch

Design: Roman Dzivulskiy
Client: TIW

1

2

3

4

5

6

ART STUDIO

7. Mayak

Design: Roman Dzivulskiy
Client: Mayak

8. Kniga

Design: Roman Dzivulskiy
Client: Kniga

9. Trizio

Design: Roman Dzivulskiy
Client: Trizio

10. 7ways

Design: Roman Dzivulskiy
Client: 7ways

11. Richard Caddock

Design: Zahidul Islam
Client: Richard Caddock

12. Burger&Love

Design: kissmiklos
Client: Burger&Love

7   8

9   10

11   12

1. Arrox

Design: Esteban Oliva
Client: Arrox – Bikes Designs

2. Zoetic

Design: Noeeko Studio
Client: Zoetic

3. Olly

Design: Konrad Sybilski
Client: Emotech Ltd.

4. Artifact

Design: Alexander Morgan
Client: Artifact Apparel

5. Look Addict

Design: Noeeko Studio
Client: Look Addict

6. ATHINA GKINI

Design: pd-design studio
Client: ATHINA GKINI
fashion designer

1

2

3

4

5

6

7. Varenne

Design: Noeeko Studio
Client: Varenne

8. Two12 Studio

Design: Alaa Tameem
Client: Two Twelve Studios

9. Soccer Fuel

Design: Studio AIO
Client: Soccer Fuel

10. Dream Cake

Design: Roman Dzivulskiy
Client: Bread Kherson

VARENNE·

THE FRENCH
COOK

7

8

9

DREAM CAKE

10

1. Meal delivery service

Design: Wiktor Ares
Client: Meal delivery service

2. Igla

Design: Wiktor Ares
Client: Nikita Otchenash

3. Volga

Design: Wiktor Ares
Client: Volga

4. King suburbs

Design: Wiktor Ares
Client: Vlad Karpov

5. Superb!

Design: Jack Harvatt

6. Satan

Design: Wiktor Ares
Client: Satan

1

2

3

4

5

6

7. CETE

Design: DUNA
Client: CETE Consultoria
Telefônica

8. SV

Design: Oscar Bastidas
Client: Seguros
Venezuela – Venezuelan
Insurance Company

9. Goodnight

Design: Angelos Botsis
Client: Goodnight

10. Geoad

Design: Dušan Miletć
Client: Geoad

11. Tel-Inf

Design: Fuzz Studio
Client: Tel Inf

cete

SV

7

8

gn®

Geoad

9

10

11

1. Sea

Design: Morocho Estudio
Client: Personal Project

2. Sibling

Design: Steve Wolf
Client: Sibling

3. Petfass

Design: Morocho Estudio
Client: Petfass

4. Jazzy.pro

Design: Maciej Świerczek
Client: Jazzy Innovations

5. Sivori

Design: Morocho Estudio
Client: Personal Project

6. Ring Side Gym

Design: Studio AIO
Client: Ring Side Gym

1

2

3

5

6

GOOD GARDEN

CREATIVE LANDSCAPING IDEAS

7

FUNTIME

8

7. Good Garden

Design: Vladislav Smolkin
Client: Good Garden

8. Funtime

Design: Alexander Tsanev
Client: Funtime

9. thatcopyshop

Design: Jack Harvatt
Client: thatcopyshop

10. Sandwich

Design: Jack Harvatt

9

10

1. RBN

Design: Dušan Miletć
Client: RBN

2. BLZN

Design: Dušan Miletć
Client: Blaznevac Night Club

3. Hug Agency

Design: Variant73
Client: Hug Agency

4. YoYo

Design: Denys Kotliarov
Client: Brick technology Ltd.

5. FutureTech Team

Design: Dušan Miletć
Client: FutureTech Team

1   2

3   4

5

50 Fifty50 50

6

7

25%

Twenty Five
Percent
OFF.

FITZGERALD
KITCHENS

8

9

10

11

6. ODJO

Design: Asen Petrov
Client: ODJO

7. 50 | 50

Design: VOLTA Brand
Shaping Studio
Client: 50 | 50

8. 25% Off

Design: Asen Petrov
Client: Shopping Auction

9. Fitzgerald Kitchens

Design: Dušan Miletć
Client: Fitzgerald Kitchens

10. Aqua

Design: Denys Kotliarov
Client: Aqua

11. Halfprice

Design: Angelos Botsis
Client: Halfpricedeals

1. CMED Construction

Design: Hiromi Maeo
(enhanced Inc.)
Client: CMED
Construction Co., Ltd.

2. Kapeh – Atiplan Gold

Design: Joshua Barillas
Client: Kapeh

3. DOTO East Hokkaido Electric

Design: Hiromi Maeo
(enhanced Inc.)
Client: DOTO East Hokkaido
Electric Co., Ltd.

4. FGM3

Design: Hiromi Maeo
(enhanced Inc.)
Client: FGM3
Environmental LLC

1

2

DO|TO East Hokkaido Electric Co.,Ltd.

3

FGM3 Environmental

4

5. Composit

Design: Value Studio
(in collaboration with
AP'BRANDS)
Client: Composit

6. Talon

Design: Value Studio
in collaboration with
AP'BRANDS
Client: Talon

7. Tara

Design: Jiani Lu
Client: Tara

8. History Herrytage

Design: KR8 bureau
Client: History Herrytage

9. Eniosol

Design: KR8 bureau
Client: Eniosol e.U.

5

6

NATURE'S FORMULA

7

8

eniosol

9

1. Unshakeable Rascalsa

Design: Bo Hao Ciou
Client: Self-initiated Project

2. Sushi Express – 1

Design: Bo Hao Ciou
Client: Sushi Express

3. Sushi Express – 2

Design: Bo Hao Ciou
Client: Sushi Express

4. Special Events for Children's Day & Art Festival

Design: Bo Hao Ciou,
Meng Chieh Li

Client: Taipei Fine Arts
Museum

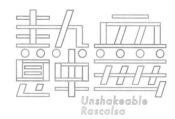

1

2

3

4

5. WHY? ART

Design: Bo Hao Ciou
Client: Self-initiated Project

6. Appreciation of Art through Dialogue

Design: Masaomi Fujita
Client: Hiratsuka
Museum of Art

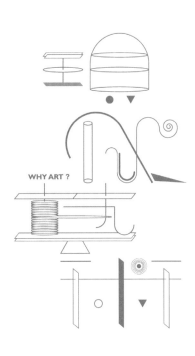

WHY ART ?

5

平塚市美術館

対話による
美術鑑賞

6

1. Vivaá

Design: Variant73
Client: Vivaá

2. DOM Logistics

Design: Variant73
Client: DOM Logistics

3. Pikaboo travel

Design: Panfilov &
Yushko Creative Group
Client: Pikaboo travel

4. 7&2 – Street Wear

Design: Dawid Cmok
Client: 7&2

5. Lab 21

Design: Filipe Guimarães
Client: Lab 21

1

2

3

4

5

6. VideoSmile

Design: Alexander Shimanov
Client: Videosmile

7. Sabotage

Design: Alexander Shimanov
Client: Sabotage

8. Rodina

Design: Alexander Shimanov
Client: Rodina

9. Zhiviem

Design: Alexander Shimanov
Client: Zhiviem

10. Football

Design: Alexander Shimanov
Client: Mother Russia

11. Vokrug sveta

Design: Alexander Shimanov
Client: Vokrug sveta

6   7

8   9

10   11

1. Zavod Battle

Design: Insando
Client: Dance school "Masta"

2. Petra Digital

Design: Noeeko Studio
Client: Petra Digital

3. LEGENDA

Design: Insando
Client: Elena Miroshnikova

4. Hard Reboot

Design: Insando
Client: Maxim Kozlov
(house dancer)

5. Chizh

Design: Insando
Client: Dmitry Chizh

6. Playfulfingers

Design: Insando
Client: Vlad Finger

1

2

3

4

4

5

6

7

8

9

10

11

12

7. Frisson

Design: Insando
Client: Vlad Finger

8. Hello B*tches

Design: Insando
Client: Alexandra Kim &
Alyona Bagirova

9. Rhymes & Punches

Design: Insando
Client: Rhymes & Punches

10. Redko

Design: Vivien Bertin
Client: Alberto Perera

11. AZAÍ

Design: Oscar Bastidas
Client: Azaí –
Natural Products

12. Illegal Factory

Design: Vivien Bertin
Client: Illegal Factory agency

1. Nitex

Design: Typemate
Client: DJ Nitex /
Logomachine

2. Amber Room

Design: Typemate
Client: Amber Shop

3. Future Outfit

Design: Typemate
Client: On-line clothing store

4. Courage Time

Design: Typemate
Client: family quests in
Saint-Petersburg

5. Soul Kitchen

Design: Typemate
Client: Soul Kitchen
Furniture workshop

6. Type Mate

Design: Typemate
Client: design studio

1

2

3

4

5

6

7

8

7. Windaloo Media

Design: Typemate
Client: Windaloo
Media / Logomachine

8. Nikita Dobrov

Design: Typemate
Client: Internet marketolog

9. Florist

Design: Typemate
Client: blog on gardening

10. Ra Family

Design: Typemate
Client: Vegan
restaurant RaFamily

9

10

1. Wisp

Design: Kimmy Lee
Client: Self-initiated Project

2. Aroma

Design: Tobias Hall
Client: Café Nero

3. Bike Story

Design: Maciej Świerczek
Client: Bike Story

4. Universal

Design: Tobias Hall
Client: Self-initiated Project

1

2

3

4

5. Jimbo

Design: Jimbo Bernaus
Client: Jimbo Bernaus

6. Knock

Design: Jimbo Bernaus
Client: Knock ws

7. Wanderlust

Design: Kimmy Lee
Client: Self-initiated Project

8. Krisbel&Co

Design: Jimbo Bernaus
Client: Krisbel&Co

Jimbo

Knock

5

6

Wanderlust

7

Krisbel & Co

8

1. Mush

Design: Wiktor Ares
Client: video
workshop "Mush"

2. Grubnero

Design: Wiktor Ares
Client: Maxim Obyedkov

3. Rocknroll

Design: Wiktor Ares
Client: Night club of
"Vmeste bar"

4. Brand-Bureau

Design: Wiktor Ares
Client: Sergei Prokofiev

5. Beast

Design: Wiktor Ares
Client: Kirill Osipov

6. Sleep

Design: Wiktor Ares
Client: A sleepless night

1

2

3

4

5

6

7. Lunar

Design: Alexander Shimanov
Client: Lunar

8. Kaiser Interier Design

Design: Dave Klimek
Client: Kaiser Jaroslav

9. RED ONE

Design: Dawid Cmok
Client: RED ONE

10. ROAK

Design: Dawid Cmok
Client: ROAK

11. Uncoded

Design: Giada Tamborrino
Client: Uncoded Events

7

8

9

10

11

1. bro.Kat

Design: Marta Gawin
Client: bro.Kat

2. Arguzzi

Design: Andrea Schlaffer
Client: Arguzzi

3. Orguyo

Design: Morocho Estudio
Client: Orguyo Theater

4. Toxpro

Design: Studio Goat
Client: Toxpro

broKat

ARGUZZ4
LAMP DESIGN

1

2

ORGUYO

3

4

5. Aira

Design: Studio Goat
Client: MullenLowe GGK

6. eyerim

Design: Studio Goat
Client: eyerim

7. 5'Oclick

Design: Typemate
Client: marketing agency /
Logomachine

8. Ranger

Design: Typemate
Client: Team of game
developers / Logomachine

5   6

ɓo'click
агентство интернет продаж

7

· RANGER ·

8

1. Roomka

Design: Dave Klimek
Client: Roomka

2. Bauhaus

Design: Asen Petrov
Client: Bauhaus

3. Decode

Design: Two Times Elliott
Client: Decode

4. Speak Easy

Design: Asen Petrov
Client: Burton

5. Ace Auto

Design: Alexander Yaguza
Client: Andrey Lyashenko

ROOMKA

bauh
aus

1   2

DECODE®

3

4   5

6. Cahri digital

Design: Studio Goat
Client: Cahri Digital

7. Warm Up

Design: Giada Tamborrino
Client: Warm Up Events

8. Silarba

Design: Another Collective
Client: Silarba

9. Zabrzańskie Graffiti

Design: Dawid Cmok
Client: Zabrzańskie Graffiti

10. The Hive

Design: Steve Wolf
Client: The Hive

CaHRI©
DIGITAL

WARM
UP

6
7

s1larba

8

ZG
ZABRZAŃSKIE
GRAFFITI .

9
10

1. Bean Bar Bite

Design: Demetris Kalambokis
Client: The Bean Bar

2. Cornware

Design: Kevin
Harald Campean
Client: Cornware

3. Sidelight

Design: Kevin
Harald Campean
Client: Sidelight

1

SIDELIGHT
PHOTO STUDIO

2

3

SPORTS BAR

CLUBE

PORTO · RUGBY

x

ONDE SE JOGA A 3ª PARTE

Elline Moda

CONFECTION

4

5

VALUE

Fridaymilk

6

7

EVNT CO.

ITS ALL ABOUT THE DAY

AP'BRANDS

8

9

4. CLUBE

Design: VOLTA Brand
Shaping Studio
Client: CLUBE

5. Elline Moda

Design: Value Studio
Client: Elline Moda

6. Value

Design: Value Studio
Client: Value Studio

7. Fridaymilk

Design: Value Studio
Client: Fridaymilk

8. EVNT CO.

Design: Angelos Botsis
Client: The Event Company

9. AP'BRANDS

Design: Value Studio
(in collaboration with
AP'BRANDS)
Client: AP'BRANDS

1. Tipologia

Design: Alexander Yaguza
Client: Tipologia studio

2. Herimeheri

Design: Angelos Botsis
Client: Herimeheri. Extra
Virgin Olive oil Products

3. Albaker

Design: Studio AIO
Client: Fahad Albaker

4. Equilibrium

Design: Noeeko Studio
Client: Equilibrium

tipologia   HERI ME HERI®

1   2

ALBAKER

3

EQUILIBR/UM

4

5. El Globo

Design: sstudio™
Client: Club
Huracan Chivilcoy

6. Lexcorp

Design: Dunia Mushcab
Client: Personal Project

7. The Hub

Design: sstudio™
Client: The Hub

8.Xiquell

Design: KR8 bureau
Client: xiquell GmbH

9. Kanica Weaving

Design: Angelos Botsis
Client: Laura Vargas Llianas

10. Intouchables

Design: Nick Zotov
Client: Personal Project

EL GLOBO   LEⅩCORP

5   6

THE HUB^{TS}   xiqûell

7   8

KANICA   Intôuchables

9   10

1. Evolve Dynamics

Design: Kimmy Lee
Client: Evolve Dynamics

2. Branch Creative

Design: Noeeko Studio
Client: Branch Creative

3. Levels Contracting EST

Design: Alaa Tameem
Client: Levels
Contracting EST

4. Fashion Course

Design: Alaa Tameem
Client: Lomar Fashion

EVOLVE

DYNAMICS

B——C

branch
creative

1

2

LEVELS// CONTRACTING
EST

3

FASHION &
HAUTE—
COUTURE
TEXTILE

4

5. La Masia

Design: sstudio™
Client: La Masia
Bar de Tapas

6. Balint Jaksa

Design: kissmiklos
Client: Balint Jaksa

7. Fuzz Studio

Design: Fuzz Studio
Client: Fuzz Studio

8. aKINO

Design: Marta Gawin
Client: Stowarzyszenie Nowe
Horyzonty

9. MAP. DFNDR

Design: Dušan Miletć
Client: MAP. DFNDR

5   6

FUZZ   aKINO

7   8

MAP.DFNDR

9

1. Art Group

Design: Pavel Saksin
Client: Art Group

2. Post 21

Design: Roberto Alba
Client: Post 21

3. Bent Taco

Design: vacaliebres
Client: Bent Taco

4. Yesno

Design: Pavel Saksin
Client: Yesno

5. Maria Pastelera

Design: Roberto Alba
Client: Maria Pastelera

6. Terra Cotta

Design: Roberto Alba
Client: Terra Cotta

1

2

3

4

5

6

L I N C O L N   E S T A T E S

7

7. Lincoln Estates

Design: Kimmy Lee
Client: Self-initiated Project

8. Lifeline

Design: Kimmy Lee
Client: Snow Click Ice Cream

9. Veggieshack

Design: Kimmy Lee
Client: Self-initiated Project

8

veggieshack

9

1. BBC Digital Studios

Design: StudioMH
Client: BBC

2. Stepan

Design: Alexander Shimanov
Client: Pavel Tinyaev

3. Personality cult

Design: Panfilov &
Yushko Creative Group
Client: Personality cult

4. Yosma

Design: Tobias Hall
Client: Here design

5. Dead russian

Design: Alexander Shimanov
Client: Dead Russian

6. BBC Music Jazz

Design: StudioMH
Client: BBC

1

Степан

2

КУЛЬТ ЛИЧНОСТИ

3

4

5

6

7. Fireworks Kingdom

Design: Typemate
Client: Online fireworks shop /
Logomachine

8. Sport

Design: Value Studio
Client: Sport

9. Baixaria

Design: VOLTA Brand
Shaping Studio
Client: Baixaria

10. Orange

Design: sstudio™
Client: Orange Agency

11. Hustle

Design: Value Studio
Client: Hustle

12. Litelee

Design: Creogram
Branding&Digital Agency
Client: Litelee

7

8

9

10

11

12

1. Love Hate

Design: Dawid Cmok
Client: Love Hate

2. SO

Design: Sean O'Connor
Client: Sean O'Connor

3. Telly

Design: Pavel Saksin
Client: Telly

4. Agali Agali

Design: Demetris Kalambokis
Client: Agali Agali

5. Big Joy

Design: Dawid Cmok
Client: Big Joy

6. Ride

Design: Roberto Alba
Client: Ride

1

2

3

4

5

6

7. Rabbit
Design: Kimmy Lee
Client: Self-initiated Project

8. ÚNICA
Design: DUNA
Client: Agência Única

9. One-2-Three
Design: Kimmy Lee
Client: Self-initiated Project

10. Bud
Design: Kimmy Lee
Client: Self-initiated Project

11. Tütü
Design: Kevin
Harald Campean
Client: Tütü

12. Lejdis Quartet
Design: Fuzz Studio
Client: Lejdis Quartet

7

8

9

10

BAR • CLUB

11

12

1. Indian Gardens

Design: Nebojsa Matkovic
Client: Indian Gardens

2. EXPO 2022 Lodz Poland Candidate City

Design: Creogram Branding&Digital Agency
Client: EXPO 2022 Lodz Poland Candidate City

3. RESULT OF BROKEN CONDOMS

Design: Kosmog
Client: RESULT OF BROKEN CONDOMS

4. TONY ROSS SALON

Design: Kosmog
Client: TONY ROSS SALON

5. The Max Burger

Design: Alexander Yaguza
Client: Maxim Mishenko

6. Taktus

Design: Angelos Botsis
Client: Taktus Creative

GARLAND'S
Indian Gardens
· CAFE & MARKET ·

1

EXPO 2022 LODZ POLAND
Candidate City

2

3

T C N Y
R O S S
SALON

4

THE
Max
BURGER

5

taktus®

6

7. Vertical Series

Design: Giada Tamborrino
Client: Vertical Series Events

8. SUSU

Design: Kevin
Harald Campean
Client: Susu

9. Basilica

Design: Kevin
Harald Campean
Client: Basilica

10. Weiss

Design: Giada Tamborrino
Client: Weiss –
Toolroom Records

**11. CoffeeDeal Distribution
Network**

Design: Cursor Design Studio
Client: Tsekouras Dionysis

12. UNNA

Design: Typemate
Client: Clothing brand
UNNA / Logomachine

7

8

9

10

11

12

1. Second Spoon

Design: Kimmy Lee
Client: Self-initiated Project

2. Ava and Eve

Design: Kimmy Lee
Client: Self-initiated Project

3. Bread & Butter

Design: Kimmy Lee
Client: Self-initiated Project

4. Vinimal

Design: Kimmy Lee
Client: Self-initiated Project

1

2

3

4

5. FFK

Design: Marta Gawin
Client: Cult Film Festival

6. M-1 Autoparts

Design: Kimmy Lee
Client: M-1 Autoparts

7. Sushiaria

Design: Another Collective
Client: Sushiaria

8. Native

Design: Kimmy Lee
Client: Self-initiated Project

Festiwal Filmów Kultowych

5

6

restaurante · sushi

7

8

1. Sugar Coated

Design: Studio AIO
Client: Sugar Coated

2. Jazz Forum

Design: Fuzz Studio
Client: None

3. ARSA

Design: Kimmy Lee
Client: Self-initiated Project

4. Rider Guide

Design: Typemate
Client: sports mobile app

5. Brain VR

Design: Sean O'Connor
Art Direction: Alex Norton
Client: MIT

1

2

3

4

Brain VR

5

6

7

8

9

**6. The Brunchery –
Brunch & More Restaurant**

Design: Demetris Kalambokis
Client: The Brunchery

7. M.W. Monogram

Design: Kimmy Lee
Client: Self-initiated Project

8. Viereck

Design: kissmiklos
Client: Viereck

9. Ferjan

Design: Studio AIO
Client: Ferjan

10. PieHvb

Design: Sean O'Connor
Client: PieHvb

PIEHṼB

10

1. MOC

Design: Marta Gawin
Client: MOC Architecture

2. IMPACT

Design: pd-design studio
Client: IMPACT
interior design studio

3. Borary

Design: FLAT12 studio
Client: Borary

4. assis business partners

Design: Another Collective
Client: assis
business partners

1

2

3

4

ZUO CORP +

5. Zuo Corp +

Design: Konrad Sybilski
Client: Zuo Corp +

6. Sushi Shop

Design: Andrea Schlaffer
Client: Sushi Shop

7. mishmash

Design: Another Collective
Client: mishmash

8. jaju

Design: Another Collective
Client: jaju

9. Momentum

Design: Kimmy Lee
Client: Self-initiated Project

5

6

mishmash®

jaju

7

8

9

1. DPS

Design: Dunia Mushcab
Client: Design Per Second

2. Go Burger

Design: Nebojsa Matkovic
Client: Go Burger

3. Cosmic Trip

Design: Creogram
Branding&Digital Agency
Client: Funktronic Labs

4. Vestite Lopez

Design: Roberto Alba
Client: Vestite Lopez

5. Snow Click

Design: Kimmy Lee
Client: Snow Click Ice Cream

6. Island Apparel

Design: Kimmy Lee
Client: Island Apparel

1

2

3

4

5

6

7

8

9

10

11

12

7. Krym

Design: Alexander Shimanov
Client: Krym

8. Glavmotor

Design: Alexander Shimanov
Client: Mother Russia

9. Tradiciya

Design: Alexander Shimanov
Client: Mother Russia

10. Rozhdennye

Design: Alexander Shimanov
Client: Rhyme borns

11. Jesus junkie

Design: Alexander Shimanov
Client: Jesus Junkie wear

12. Survivor

Design: Joshua Barillas
Client: Survivor

1. Mikros Borias

Design: Angelos Botsis
Client: Mikros Borias

2. P. Pollito

Design: Andrea Pinter

3. Le Sechoir

Design: Studio AIO
Client: Le Sechoir

4. Spaghettata

Design: Giada Tamborrino
Client: Spaghettata
Restaurant

1

2

3

4

5. AK

Design: Value Studio
Client: Andrey Kalyuzhnyi

6. Gorkassa

Design: Typemate
Client: Online payment
system Gorkassa

7. Baldoria

Design: Another Collective
Client: Baldoria

8. Sunlight village

Design: Typemate
Client: Sunlight village

9. Postcard

Design: Typemate
Client: Postcard.travel

5   6

GARRAFEIRA ✕ BAR

7   8

9

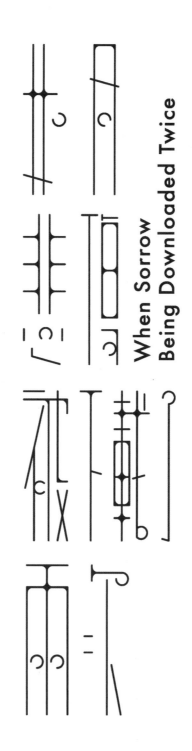

When Sorrow
Being Downloaded Twice

1

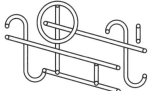

2

3

4

5

6

1. When Sorrow Being Downloaded Twice

Design: Bo Hao Ciou
Client: Self-initiated Project

2. Idealform – 1

Design: Bo Hao Ciou,
Meng Chieh Li
Client: Idealform

3. Idealform – 2

Design: Bo Hao Ciou,
Meng Chieh Li
Client: Idealform

4. Beitou Heterotopia

Design: Bo Hao Ciou
Client: Idealform

5. Hung Yun Color Printing

Design: Bo Hao Ciou,
Meng Chieh Li
Client: Hung Yun
Color Printing

6. Secret

Design: Bo Hao Ciou
Client: Oriental
Institute of Technology

1. 605 10th Ave

Design: sstudio™
Client: 605 10th Ave

2. ARCADE

Design: sstudio™
Client: Arcade

3. WLW Group

Design: Studio Goat
Client: WLW Group

4. Utrennik

Design: Dock 57
Client: "Utrennik"
Morning parties

5. Líquida

Design: sstudio™
Client: Líquida Comunicación

6. Mangram

Design: sstudio™
Client: Mangram

1

2

3

4

5

6

SYMBOL & TYPE

For most logo designers, the combination of image and text is always a reliable option. Using a literal message makes it easy to clarify the brand's information directly, which allows the audience to more easily grasp the visual characteristics of the company's identification. This solution is widely practiced, making it vital to explore new directions when using it to suggest freshness and creativity in the long term.

The Interview with
UDS

*by **Alexander Tsanev***

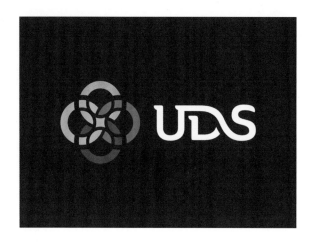

1. How do you find a concept for a new logo project?

There is no a ready formula for finding a concept for a new logo. Just try to keep your mind open and inspiration could come from anywhere.

2. When you start to work on a logo, what are the steps involved usually?

For completing a successful logo design project I try to stick to the following design process:

– **The Creative Brief.** Probably one of the most important steps in a logo project is to accumulate initial information from the client about their project and needs. This could be done by a face to face interview or via questionnaire. Without a good understanding of the project specifics, you should avoid starting a logo project. Just try to gather as much information as you can. This will definitely be useful in the next steps.

– **Research.** After gathering enough information from the brief, the next crucial step is the research phase. The research could include general reading on the industry itself, its history, major competitors, etc.

Research is a critical phase for every logo design project as it ensures that your logo will differ from the competitors. It also sets a good benchmark. You can use the results from your research when you present your design concepts.

Sometimes it is helpful to perform some initial visual research, too. This is not research into the client's business but on the actual logo style, approach or attitude.

– **Sketching and Design.** Using the design brief and the research results, start developing the first logo design concepts. I always try to begin with quick exploration sketches and see if a particular idea works or not. Do not limit yourself in this stage. Take as much time as you need and explore as many possible directions as you can. Remember that there is no such thing as a bad idea, just bad decisions.

After picking up the best concepts, go a step further and vectorize them. Try to work only in black and white first, then when you are happy with the outcome, play with typography and colors.

– **Presentation.** Another important step in the project. You must be able to explain to the client the design decisions that you made. I personally present only the best three concepts.

– **Fine-tuning and Project Files Delivery.** After several design rounds of further explorations and fine tuning, hopefully the client is happy and ready to pick the best logo concept. The last step in the logo project is preparing the files for the final delivery.

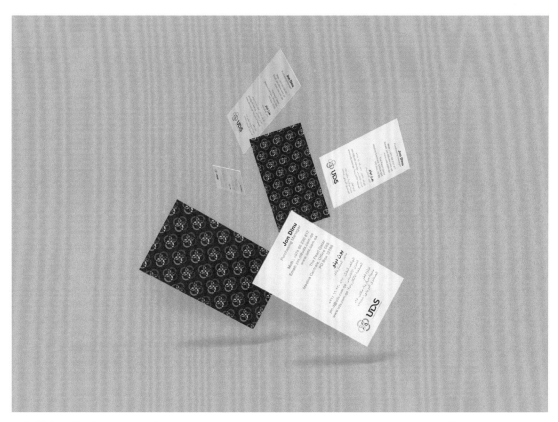

3. What message do you want the logo "UDS" to convey to the audience who views it?

UDS is a European company willing to open offices in Qatar, Middle East. They offer different services ranging from interior design solutions to 3D visualizations, architecture, and furniture production. The project goal was developing the overall branding and positioning the company as a creative and trustworthy partner in the new market. The challenge was to present UDS in a way that will relate to the local perceptions.

The concept behind the logo represents a union of four circles that form the overall symbol. Each of these circles stands for one of the company's core services — interior design, 3D visualizations, architecture, and product design. To highlight this concept, the logo also uses a combination of four different colors forming a mosaic image similar to those prevalent in

Islamic traditional art. The typographic part was developed from scratch and uses curved shapes to make sure that it is a perfect match next to the symbol. The logo was well received by the local audience, who recognize in it a familiar and trustworthy company image.

4. What is the most challenging part about logo design and how do you deal with it?

Each of us is bombarded by more than a hundred logos on a daily basis. Probably the most challenging part for a logo designer is to come up with a unique and fresh idea. Always try to be as creative as your project or client allows you to be.

5. What makes a good logo in your opinion?

Simple, memorable and unique solutions make a logo work in the long run.

6. What is your suggestion to young logo designers?

Always try to learn and improve. Work hard but don't be too hard to yourself, especially in the first years of your career. And remember, practice makes you a better designer. Good luck!

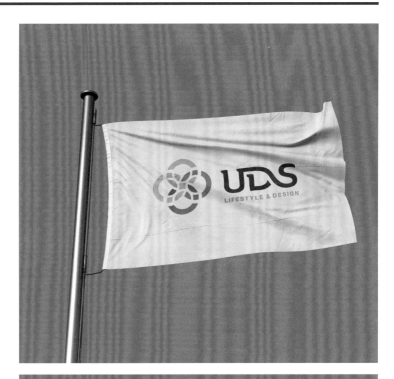

1. Mr. Tooth

Design: Dawid Cmok
Client: Mr. Tooth

2. Human &
Art Photography

Design: Fuzz Studio
Client: Human & Art
Monika Wypych

3. Keeunit

Design: Alexander Tsanev
Client: Keeunit

4. We Know Users

Design: Abstract Logic
Client: Berkan Ozden

5. Omnium

Design: Alexander Tsanev
Client: Omnium

6. Skiworld

Design: Alexander Morgan
Client: Skiworld

1   2

3   4

5   6

7. Mind Digger

Design: Kreatank
Client: Sergey Sobolev

8. ELYT renewable energy sources

Design: POSITIVE designlab
Client: Lazaros Sofikitis

9. Akant

Design: Maciej Świerczek
Client: Akant

10. Fondeo

Design: Misael Osorio
Client: Fondeo

11. Blender

Design: Maciej Świerczek

12. PORTECONOMICS

Design: pd-design studio
Client: PORTECONOMICS

7

8

9

10

11

12

1. Bird Nest

Design: Zahidul Islam
Client: Bird Nest

2. Extra Virgin Olive Oil

Design: Zahidul Islam
Client: Extra Virgin Olive Oil

3. The Voyage Club

Design: Zahidul Islam
Client: The Voyage Club

4. Maylas Fenyal

Design: Studio AIO
Client: Maylas Fenyal

5. Cathedral

Design: Dawid Cmok
Client: Cathedral

1

2

3

4

5

6

7

6. Catering

Design: Abstract Logic
Client: Crew Catering

7. The Koko Tree

Design: Studio AIO
Client: The Koko Tree

8. Royalty Services

Design: Alexander Tsanev
Client: Royalty Services

9. Arcus

Design: Kreatank
Client: Jessie Seigel

10. Hamad Alobiadan Development of Real Estate Investment

Design: Carving Studio
Client: Hamad Alobiadan Development of real estate investment

11. Sofia Luxury Residence

Design: Alexander Tsanev
Client: Hype Digital Agency

8

9

10

11

1. Cosmos Ocean

Design: Luminous
Design Group

Client: Cosmos Ocean /
Sea Groupage

2. Prosper IQ

Design: Steve Wolf

Client: Prosper IQ

3. Highlands Engineering

Design: The Office of
Visual Communication

Client: Highlands Engineering

1

2

3

4. Juxta Connections

Design: Alexander Morgan
Client: Juxta Connections

5. Medical Tourism

Design: Misael Osorio
Client: Buró de
convenciones y visitantes

6. Lepsza Woda

Design: Aleksandra
Godlewska
Client: ARM Lepsza Woda

7. Munich

Design: Panfilov & Yushko
Creative Group
Client: Munich

8. United Scrubs of America

Design: The Office of
Visual Communication
Client: United Scrubs
of America

4

5

6

7

8

1. Iron Lion

Design: Inluw Team
Client: Iron Lion

2. Sova

Design: FLAT12 studio
Client: Sova

3. Azumami

Design: Studio AIO
Client: Azumami

4. Tiffin Farms

Design: Studio AIO
Client: Tiffin Farms

1

2

3

4

5. Wagashi

Design: Marta Śleszyńska
Client: Student Project

**6. Sgt. Martinho –
torrefatora lisboeta**

Design: vacaliebres
Client: Sgt. Martinho

7. Lé-chon

Design: Misael Osorio
Client: Lé-Chon Foodtruck

8. Molli

Design: Studio AIO
Client: Molli

9. Frozen World LTD

Design: Demetris Kalambokis
Client: Frozen Products store

10. Welcome

Design: FLAT12 studio
Client: Welcome

5

6

7

8

9

10

1. Healthy way of living

Design: Kamila Figura
Client: healthy way of living blog

2. Flowly

Design: Abstract Logic
Client: Ivan Klimov

3. Maki

Design: Alaa Tameem
Client: Maki Restaurant

4. The Fries

Design: Alaa Tameem
Client: The fries restaurant

5. Beautify the city!

Design: Abstract Logic
Client: Beautify the city!

6. Amorales

Design: FLAT12 studio
Client: Amorales

1

2

3

4

5

6

7. Shrimp Box

Design: Alaa Tameem
Client: Shrimp Box Restaurant

8. Sudperle

Design: Kreatank
Client: Joana Marie Karger

9. Novoyanino

Design: FLAT12 studio
Client: Novoyanino

10. MiniCoffee

Design: FLAT12 studio
Client: Minicoffee

11. The Palace Painters

Design: Zahidul Islam
Client: The Palace Painters

12. Kickstand

Design: Stefan Grubačić
Client: Kickstand Ice Cream

7

8

9

10

11

12

1. The Colony

Design: Studio AIO
Client: The Colony

2. Masar

Design: Studio AIO
Client: Masar

3. Alqadeeri

Design: Studio AIO
Client: Alqadeeri

4. Fontaine Marketing

Design: The Office of
Visual Communication
Client: Fontaine Marketing

5. Tiny Picks

Design: Studio AIO
Client: Tiny Picks

6. Head Space

Design: Studio AIO
Client: Head Space

1

2

3

4

5

6

7

8

9

10

11

12

7. Manaslu

Design: Maciej Świerczek
Client: Manaslu

8. Pussy Lover

Design: Dawid Cmok
Client: Pussy Lover

9. Bfit

Design: Studio AIO
Client: Bfit

10. Newport Race

Design: Zahidul Islam
Client: Newport Race

11. Warehouse 23

Design: Studio AIO
Client: Warehouse 23

12. Cute Jars

Design: Studio AIO
Client: Cute Jars

1. ONIS

Design: Stefan Grubačić
Client: Onis International

2. Greek Basket

Design: Luminous
Design Group
Client: Greek Basket /
Supply & Demand

3. VR PROJECT

Design: pd-design studio
Client: VR PROJECT

4. ENQU

Design: Kamila Figura
Client: ENQU

5. Skiathos Blu

Design: Luminous
Design Group
Client: Skiathos Blu /
Luxury Hotel

6. Leontiadis Family

Design: Luminous
Design Group
Client: Leontiadis Family /
Bakery Products

1

2

3

4

5

6

7

8

7. Meritas –
interior designer

Design: John Soultanidis
Client: Vassilis Meritas

8. RTA –
certification experts

Design: POSITIVE designlab
Client: RTA – Real Time Audit

9. Vitrage, Estudio De Arte

Design: Andrea Pinter

10. Eleni
Trikatsoula

Design: Demetris Kalambokis
Client: Eleni Trikatsoula

11. Great Thinkers Group

Design: Variant73
Client: Great Thinkers Group

12. Algoducci

Design: Variant73
Client: Algoducci

9

10

11

12

1. Hop Napalm

Design: Roman Dzivulskiy
Client: Hop Napalm

2. Bread Kherson

Design: Roman Dzivulskiy
Client: Bread Kherson

3. Lollo Rosso

Design: Radmir Volk
Client: Lollo Rosso

4. Wow things

Design: Typemate
Client: information
resource of new
technologies and inventions

5. L'assassino Restaurant

Design: POSITIVE designlab
Client: L'assassino restaurant

6. Finger Sushi

Design: Studio AIO
Client: Finger Sushi

1

2

3

4

5

1. European Field Archery Championships 2015

Design: Fuzz Studio
Client: Polish
Archery Federation

2. Spaceman

Design: Dock 57
Client: Personal project

3. MPM Projects

Design: Abstract Logic
Client: MPM Projects

4. FOOD GALLERY

Design: pd–design studio
Client: food gallery

5. 2b – Bio & Beauty

Design: Maurizio Pagnozzi
Client: 2b – Bio & Beauty

6. Stark Gaming

Design: Andrea Pinter

1

2

3

4

5

6

7

8

7. BG Commerce

Design: Stefan Grubačić
Client: BG Commerce

8. Brain Waves

Design: Stefan Grubačić
Client: Brain Waves

9. Velocity cycle club

Design: Dock 57
Client: Personal project

10. Shift

Design: Studio AIO
Client: Shift Media
Productions

11. CAPE

Design: Stefan Grubačić
Client: Cape Racing Yachts

12. Seven Citizen

Design: Carving Studio
Client: Seven Citizen

VELOCITY
CYCLE CLUB

9

10

11

12

1. Roca de Ayuda

Design: Joshua Barillas
Client: Iglesia Roca de Ayuda

2. Santxo

Design: Joshua Barillas
Client: Calzado La Palma

**3. Ministerios Ebenezer
Guatemala**

Design: Joshua Barillas
Client: Ministerios
Ebenezer Guatemala

4. Ava Motors

Design: Joshua Barillas
Client: Ava Motors

5. Finstack

Design: Esteban Oliva
Client: Finstack –
Sepa Direct Debit

6. Semana de Bendición

Design: Joshua Barillas
Client: Iglesia Puertas de
Restauración

1

2

3

4

5

6

7. Brainy

Design: Value Studio
Client: Brainy

8. Snowrider

Design: Value Studio
(in collaboration with
AP'BRANDS)
Client: Snowrider

9. RosInterMarketing

Design: Value Studio
Client: RosInterMarketing

10. Hotspot Tours

Design: VOLTA Branding
Shaping Studio
Client: Hotspot Tours

11. Yottly

Design: Zivan Rosic
Client: Yottly

7   8

9

10   11

1. Via Citrus

Design: Steve Wolf
Client: Via Citrus

2. Cubo Coffee

Design: Esteban Oliva
Client: Cubo Coffee

3. Patisserie Kei

Design: Masaomi Fujita
Client: Patisserie Kei

4. BTZ Group

Design: Studio AIO
Client: BTZ Group

5. DrumStarz

Design: FLAT12 studio
Client: Drumstarz

6. Sniff Inn

Design: Botond Vörös
Client: Sniff Inn

1

2

3

4

5

6

7. Split

Design: Kamila Figura
Client: Split

8. Donut House

Design: Andrea Schlaffer
Client: Donut House

9. Flamingo

Design: Dawid Cmok
Client: Flamingo

10. Sandix

Design: Esteban Oliva
Client: Sandix –
Digital Solutions Group

11. Baltic Airport

Design: Dawid Cmok
Client: Baltic Airport

12. Sparka

Design: Studio AIO
Client: Sparka

Split

DONUT
HOUSE.

7

8

Flamingo.

SANDIX
SOLUTIONS

9

10

Baltic Airport

SPARKA

11

12

1. Aperture

Design: Inluw Team
Client: Aperture

2. Kawa

Design: Masaomi Fujita
Client: Coffeenity Limited
Hong Kong

**3. Mastos – jams &
spoon sweets**

Design: POSITIVE designlab
Client: Ouli Georgia

4. Brave

Design: Andrea Schlaffer
Client: Brave

5. Jeel

Design: Studio AIO
Client: Jeel

6. Flip & CO

Design: Morocho Estudio
Client: Personal Project

1

2

3

4

5

6

7

8

9

10

11

12

7. Olives.co

Design: Alexander Morgan
Client: Olives.co

8. Vous.Me

Design: Stefan Grubačić
Client: Vous.Me

9. MAMAJUANA

Design: CHOCOTOY
Client: MAMAJUANA

10. KALIVIS S.A.

Design: pd-design studio
Client: KALIVIS S.A.

11. Bonaci

Design: Dock 57
Client: Bonaci seafood brand

12. Strip Republic

Design: Studio AIO
Client: Strip Republic

1. Huntington Beach State Park

Design: Daniel Owen Comite
Client: South Carolina State Parks

2. Bicycle City Studios

Design: Jack Harvatt
Client: Bicycle City Studios

3. Poetic Papers

Design: Jack Harvatt
Client: Poetic Papers

4. Antebellum Iron Mansion

Design: Daniel Owen Comite
Client: Antebellum Iron Mansion

5. Savannah Beach Inn

Design: Daniel Owen Comite
Client: Savannah Beach Inn

6. Swaddle & Sling

Design: Daniel Owen Comite
Client: Swaddle & Sling

1

2

3

4

5

6

7. Gulp

Design: Jack Harvatt
Client: Personal Project

8. Far Fetched Creations

Design: Jack Harvatt
Client: Far Fetched Creations

9. Rambling Rose

Design: Jack Harvatt
Client: Rambling Rose

10. Cold Quay

Design: Jack Harvatt
Client: UN:IK clothing

11. Mobovida

Design: Jack Harvatt
Client: Mobovida

12. Swoon

Design: Jack Harvatt
Client: Swoon

7

8

9

10

11

12

1. Special Events for Children's Day & Art Festival – 1

Design: Bo Hao Ciou, Meng Chieh Li

Client: Taipei Fine Arts Museum

2. Special Events for Children's Day & Art Festival – 2

Design: Bo Hao Ciou, Meng Chieh Li

Client: Taipei Fine Arts Museum

1

2

Sound
Waves . 2016

cursor design studio

3

4

5

6

7

8

3. **Sailor Clothes**
Design: Noeeko Studio
Client: Sailor Clothes

4. **Electrowave**
Design: Daria Stetsenko
Client: Electrowave
(Non-profit radio station)

5. **Sound Waves**
Design: Noeeko Studio
Client: Sound Waves

6. **Cursor Design Studio**
Design: Cursor Design Studio
Client: Cursor Design Studio

7. **Game Changer – series of
high profile conferences**
Design: Cursor Design Studio
Client: Media24 Group

8. **Marine**
Design: Cursor Design Studio
Client: Marine sea.bar.food
(Kotrotsios Dimitrios)

1. Barber Hall

Design: Vladislav Smolkin
Client: Barber Hall

2. Great Launch

Design: Vladislav Smolkin
Client: Great Launch

3. Esterra – Olive Goods

Design: Chris Trivizas
Client: Terra Farm

**4. Cookoovaya –
Wise Cuisine**

Design: Chris Trivizas
Client: Cookoovaya

**5. Andriotis –
Greek Olive Oil**

Design: Chris Trivizas
Client: D. & G.
Andriotis & Sia OE

6. Katamaya – Bakery

Design: Chris Trivizas
Client: Katamaya

1

2

3

4

5

6

7. Love Games

Design: Vladislav Smolkin
Client: Love Games

8. Campland

Design: Vladislav Smolkin
Client: Campland

**9. Simandiraki –
Traditional Foods**

Design: Chris Trivizas,
George Strouzas
Client: Simandiraki P. & Co.

**10. 10. Travolta –
Fish Tavern**

Design: Chris Trivizas
Client: Travolta

11. Kuero – Concierge

Design: Chris Trivizas
Client: Yannis Zerbas

**12. Kuziniera –
Pasta Corfiana**

Design: Chris Trivizas
Client: Kuziniera

LOVE GAMES

CAMPLAND

7

8

Σημανδηράκη

ΚΡΗΤΙΚΑ ΕΔΕΣΜΑΤΑ

τραβόλτα

ΨΑΡΟΤΑΒΕΡΝΑ

9

10

KUERO

CONCIERGE

KUZINIERA

PASTA CORFIANA

11

12

1. Eufloria

Design: Kimmy Lee
Client: Self-initiated Project

2. Smartguide

Design: Andrea Pinter

3. Property Force

Design: Anna Kuts
Client: Property Force

4. Retail Design Blog

Design: kissmiklos
Client: Retail Design Blog

5. Pettirosso Handcraft

Design: vacaliebres
Client: Pettirosso Handcraft

6. Filema Rodion

Design: Luminous
Design Group
Client: Filema Rodion /
Traditional Sweets

1

2

3

4

5

6

7. Music dog

Design: Vladislav Smolkin
Client: Music dog

8. Coffee Bird

Design: Vladislav Smolkin
Client: Coffee Bird

9. Let Me See

Designer: Maciej Świerczek
Client: Let Me See

10. ForRest

Design: Abstract Logic
Client: ForRest –
Handmade cafe

11. Pull&Bear

Design: Marco Oggian
Client: Pull&Bear

12. MOON FOX

Design: Oscar Bastidas
Client: Moon Fox –
Women's Luxury Lingerie

7

9

10

11

12

1. Little Drop

Design: Anna Kuts
Client: Bigdrop

2. Rokovoko

Design: Sean O'Connor
Client: Rokovoko

3. Jeddah University

Design: Alaa Tameem
Client: Jeddah University

4. Meras Investment

Design: Alaa Tameem
Client: Meras Investment

**5. Global
Dimension Consultant**

Design: Alaa Tameem
Client: Overhaul

6. Claudio Rorato Lawyers

Design: Variant73
Client: Claudio Rorato

1

2

3

4

5

6

7. Rare Collectibles TV

Design: Anna Kuts
Client: Rare Collectibles TV

8. Property Force

Design: Anna Kuts
Client: Property Force

9. Instamacro

Design: Anna Kuts
Client: Instamacro

10. Hudprom Loft

Design: Anna Kuts
Client: KSADA

**11. Waterfall
Wicking Technology**

Design: Sean O'Connor
Client: Janji

7

8

9

10

11

1. Khrysalis

Design: Kimmy Lee
Client: Self-initiated Project

2. Genty

Design: Radmir Volk
Client: Genty parfumes

3. TARATSA

Design: Cursor Design Studio
Client: TARATSA

4. Plastic Pals

Design: Kimmy Lee
Client: Self-initiated Project

5. Kgep

Design: Another Collective
Client: Kgep

6. Onetouchpoint

Design: Kimmy Lee
Client: Onetouchpoint

1

2

3

4

5

6

7. Barrel House Z
Design: Sean O'Connor &
Ethan Blouin
Art Direction: GrayMatter
Client: Barrel House Z

8. Habitat
Design: Kimmy Lee
Client: Self-initiated Project

9. Latteria
Design: Typemate
Client: Coffee shop
in St-Petersburg

10. Sesto Senso
Design: Giada Tamborrino
Client: Sesto Senso
Parrucchieri

11. Reproduction
Design: Kamila Figura
Client: Reproduction
Advertising Agency

12. Phee
Design: Luminous
Design Group
Client: Phee /
Seagrass Products

BARREL HOUSE Z

7

8

sestosenso

PARRUCCHIERI

9

10

REPRODUCTION

PHEE

11

12

1. Photo Factory

Design: Cursor Design Studio
Client: Tilemachos Gioglaris

2. RCreative

Design: Matteo Orilio
Client: Ruggiero Carmine

3. SCS

Design: Marta Gawin
Client: Stretch
Ceiling Solutions

4. Catarina Oliveira

Design: Another Collective
Client: Catarina Oliveira

5. Alpokaqua

Design: kissmiklos
Client: Alpokaqua

1

2

3

4

5

6

7

6. Klubogaleria SARP

Design: Marta Gawin
Client: Association of Polish
Architects Club and Gallery

7. Giraffe

Design: Dawid Cmok
Client: Giraffe

8. MCN Trade

Design: Marta Gawin
Client: MCN Trade

9. Silvia Brna

Design: Studio Goat
Client: Silvia Brna Architect

10. refresher

Design: Studio Goat
Client: refresher

8

9

10

1. Zippy Hippo

Design: Daniel
Bodea Kreatank
Client: Serge B

2. Aves

Design: Kreatank
Client: Bryan Tarn

3. Inti Provisions

Design: Steve Wolf
Client: Inti Provisions

4. Orphan

Design: Kreatank
Client: Julia Edwards

5. Black Fox

Design: Daria Stetsenko
Client: Black Fox —
Coffeehouse

6. Tusker Coffee

Design: Giada Tamborrino
Client: Tusker Coffee

1

2

3

4

5

6

BLACK
PANTHER

MINI HOTEL

7

8

9

CASTLE ROOK

10

11

12

7. Black Panther

Design: Vladislav Smolkin
Client: Black Panther

8. Gympo

Design: Vladislav Smolkin
Client: Gympo

9. Frost Output

Design: Kreatank
Client: Rick Frost

10. Castle Rook

Design: Stefan Grubačić
Client: Castle Rook

11. Net Hunter

Design: Vladislav Smolkin
Client: Net Hunter

12. Hanker

Design: Another Collective
Client: Hanker

1. SISTERS GOSSIP CAFE

Design: Carving Studio
Client: SISTERS
GOSSIP CAFE

2. Brutal

Design: Zivan Rosic
Client: Brutalist Architecture
Conference Series

3. Worksquarz

Design: Anna Kuts
Client: Worksquarz

4. The Weiss Group, LLP

Design: Kimmy Lee
Client: The Weiss Group, LLP

1

2

3

4

5

6

5. Discommon

Design: Sean O'Connor
Client: Discommon

6. Scoop

Design: Luminous
Design Group
Client: Scoop /
Coffee – Eatery

7. Raw Fairies

Design: Konrad Sybilski
Client: Raw Fairies

8. EXPO GATE

Design: Marco Oggian
Client: EXPO

9. King Landscape

Design: Anna Kuts
Client: King Landscape

7

8

9

1. MrHovobta

Design: Noeeko Studio
Client: MrHovobta

2. La Comisaría

Design: Henríquez
Lara Estudio
Client: La Comisaría

3. Primus

Design: kissmiklos
Client: Primus

1

2

3

NEW WAVE

Xanadu.
Gallery &
Auction
House

4

5

MATHIEU BELEN
ARCHI DESIGN

ATHENS

BESPOKE

SARTOR

6

7

Filharmonia
Łódzka
im. Artura
Rubinsteina

8

9

4. New Wave Hotel

Design: Kamila Figura
Client: New Wave Hotel

5. XANADU GALLERY

Design: OSOM STUDIOS
Client: XANADU GALLERY.

6. Mathieu Belen

Design: Vivien Bertin
Client: Mathieu Belen

7. Sartor

Design: Luminous
Design Group
Client: Sartor /
Bespoke Tailoring

**8. Arthur Rubinstein
Philharmonic**

Design: Konrad Sybilski
Client: Arthur Rubinstein
Philharmonic

9. Belle Journée

Design: Demetris Kalambokis
Client: Boule et Gaufre
(Waffle on-the-go)

1. Bonjour Appetit

Design: Demetris Kalambokis
Client: Boule et Gaufre
(Waffle on-the-go)

**2. Krackerjack – Artist
Management**

Design: Giada Tamborrino
Client: Krackerjack

3. Spotmap

Design: Typemate
Client: Sports mobile app /
Logomachine

4. One Two Team

Design: Anna Kuts
Client: One Two Team

5. Fantasyum

Design: Typemate
Client: Children's
education channel

6. Nomad Bistro

Design: Studio AIO
Client: Nomad Bistro

1

2

3

4

5

6

BY TRADITION

- GREECE -

KOLIONASIOS®

7

8

PEGGY'S POINT
LIGHTHOUSE

HERBACEOUS
DRINKS

9

10

11

12

**7. Kolionasios
Greek Baklava**

Design: Luminous
Design Group
Client: Kolionasios
Greek Baklava

8. Time Flowers

Design: Radmir Volk

9. Peggy's Point, Lighthouse

Design: Andrea Pinter

10. Herbaceous Drinks

Design: vacaliebres
Client: Pernod Ricard Italia

11. La Filoxera

Design: Henríquez
Lara Estudio
Client: Sótano 2

12. Sótano 2

Design: Henríquez
Lara Estudio
Client: Sótano 2

**1. Kinglike –
Travel & Concierge**

Design: Chris Trivizas
Client: Athanasios Mougios

2. Naga Siren

Design: Dunia Mushcab
Client: Personal Project

3. Pangea Clothing Co.

Design: Kimmy Lee
Client: Pangea Clothing Co.

4. Head Space

Design: Kimmy Lee
Client: Head Space

5. VKUS

Design: Start Lab
Client: VKUS

6. Rosk

Design: Henríquez
Lara Estudio
Client: Rosk

1

2

3

4

5

6

7

8

9

10

11

12

7. The song flows

Design: Wiktor Ares
Client: Vmeste bar

8. Scribbles

Design: Kimmy Lee
Client: Self-initiated Project

**9. Lukas
Strociak Retouching**

Design: Noeeko Studio
Client: Lukas Strociak
Retouching

10. Diamond Price Guide

Design: Anna Kuts
Client: Diamond Price Guide

**11. Sculpture
in Open Spaces**

Design: Sean O'Connor
Client: Sculpture
in Open Spaces

12. King Landscape

Design: Anna Kuts
Client: King Landscape

1. Awan for construction

Design: Carving Studio
Client: Awan for construction

2. Aldeyar Alarabiya

Design: Carving Studio
Client: Aldeyar Alarabiya

3. Alata Stud

Design: Carving Studio
Client: Alata Stud

4. Carving Studio

Design: Carving Studio
Client: Carving Studio

5. MAGNIT

Design: pd-design studio
Client: MAGNIT fashion

6. Dos Tacos

Design: Dock 57
Client: Doc Tacos street food

1

2

3

4

5

6

7. HEKAYA Arabic Perfumes

Design: Carving Studio
Client: Hekaya
Arabic Perfumes

8. Any Tea

Design: Konrad Sybilski
Client: Any Tea

9. Factory Man

Design: Noeeko Studio
Client: Factory Man

10. Duals

Design: Dock 57
Client: Duals social project

H E K A Y H

7

8

9

10

1. Akkadian

Design: Zivan Rosic
Client: Akkadian
Technology Consultancy

2. HES

Design: Creogram
Branding&Digital Agency
Client: HES

3. Delta Eight

Design: Zivan Rosic
Client: Delta Eight

4. Hugo

Design: Zivan Rosic
Client: Hugo

5. March Studio

Design: Zivan Rosic
Client: March Studio

6. The Antarctic Office

Design: Zivan Rosic
Client: The Antarctic
Office New Zealand

1

2

3

4

5

6

7

8

7. Octaeggdron

Design: Filipe Guimarães
Client: Filipe Guimarães

8. Ars Independent Festival

Design: Marta Gawin
Client: Ars
Independent Festival

9. Chili Corp

Design: Nebojsa Matkovic
Client: Brabazon

10. Fairisle Coffee Co.

Design: Steve Wolf
Client: Fairisle Coffee Co.

11. Autor Rooms

Design: Konrad Sybilski
Client: Autor Rooms

12. Airluxe

Design: Steve Wolf
Client: Airluxe

9

10

11

12

1. Dr Marmol

Design: Marta Gawin
Client: Dariusz
Marmol Dentistry

2. Joshua Barillas

Design: Joshua Barillas
Client: Joshua Barillas

3. The Infraction

Design: Value Studio
Client: The Infraction

4. Estância de Madeiras

Design: Another Collective
Client: Estância de Madeiras

1

2

3

4

ДЖЕМИКРЕМ

ПЕКАРНЯ

CUCINA

bistro

5

6

EST. 2015

BAKE & PRALINE

ATELIER DESSERTS

NOOCITY

ECOLOGIA URBANA

7

8

9

5. Jam&Cream

Design: Panfilov & Yushko
Creative Group
Client: Jam&Cream

6. Cucina Bistro

Design: Studio AIO
Client: Cucina Bistro

7. Bake & Praline

Design: Luminous
Design Group
Client: Bake & Praline /
Atelier Desserts

8. Noocity

Design: Another Collective
Client: Noocity

9. New Century Plus

Design: Value Studio
Client: New Century Plus

1. Wolfpack Striders

Design: Daniel Owen Comite
Client: Wolfpack Striders

2. Conservation Apex

Design: Daniel Owen Comite
Client: Conservation Apex
South Africa

3. Noisy Tenants

Design: Nebojsa Matkovic
Client: Noisy Tenants

4. Collingwood Crossfit

Design: Nebojsa Matkovic
Client: Joshua Chromis

5. Infamous Publisher

Design: Botond Vörös
Client: Hungarian
University of Fine Arts

6. K Regrind

Design: Value Studio
Client: K Regrind

1

2

3

4

5

6

7

8

brandingpanda

9

10

NEW
CREW
CLUB

OWLS BOOK

11

12

7. SERIOUS COW

Design: Oscar Bastidas
Client: Serious Cow – Greek
Yogurt Franchise in Florida

8. Hemato-Onco Runners

Design: Joshua Barillas
Client: Hemato-Onco Run

9. Barba Bird

Design: Dawid Cmok
Client: Barba Bird

10. Branding Panda

Design: Zahidul Islam
Client: Branding Panda

11. NIKE NEW CREW CLUB

Design: OSOM STUDIOS
Client: NIKE NEW
CREW CLUB

12. Owls Book

Design: Dawid Cmok
Client: Owls Book

1. Hungarikum

Design: Botond Vörös
Client: Ministry of Rural Development

2. Dynamic Digital

Design: Daria Stetsenko
Client: Dynamic Digital (Advertising agency)

3. TideRock Real Estate

Design: Daniel Owen Comite
Client: TideRock Management Real Estate

4. Vins

Design: Angelos Botsis
Client: Vins Enotrourism

5. FALCON

Design: Start Lab
Client: FALCON

6. Summer Sound

Design: Roman Dzivulskiy
Client: Summer Sound

1

2

3

4

5

6

HIDE & SEEK

JUSTVILLAS
FINE RESIDENCES

7

8

KAYAK
HALL OF FASHION

AURA
ORGANICS

9

10

AERO INVESTMENT

LAZZARO maglietta

11

12

7. HIDE & SEEK

Design: Insando
Client: Niberry Group

8. Justvillas –
Fine Residences

Design: Chris Trivizas
Client: George Koulouris

9. KAYAK Hall of Fashion

Design: Cursor Design Studio
Client: Kokkovas Vasilios

10. Aura Organics

Design: Cursor Design Studio
Client: Margaritopoulos
Christos

11. Aero Investment

Design: Creogram
Branding&Digital Agency
Client: Aero Investment

12. Lazzaro Maglietta

Design: Cursor Design Studio
Client: Ladopoulos Lazaros

1. Rioeddy – Endless River

Design: vacaliebres
Client: Rioeddy

2. Kampfire

Design: Kevin Harald
Campean
Client: Kampfire

**3. Private Studio Natalia
Latsinnikova**

Design: Panfilov &
Yushko Creative Group
Client: Private Studio
Natalia Latsinnikova

**4. Negative Horizon – The
5th Taiwan International
Video Art Exhibition 2016**

Design: Bo Hao Ciou,
Meng Chieh Li
Client: Hong-gah Museum

5. Brucken im Kiez

Design: Marta Gawin
Client: Stiftung
Brandenburger Tor

1 2

3 4

5

FORM

One of the most important requirements of logo design is to show the target identity in a clear and concise manner. Geometric forms, with their unique and distinctive visual features, can well achieve this effect. Whether two-dimensional shapes like circles, triangles, squares and polygons, or three-dimensional forms like cubes, pyramids, tetrahedrons and polyhedrons, they all express a dynamic aesthetic through their simple and succinct appearance.

The Interview with
GIALOUSIS

*by **Luminous Design Group***

1. Where do you typically look for inspiration?

Our source of inspiration varies from time to time. Inspiration can come from different stimulations and at different occasions. You can find inspiration surfing the net late at night, or during a night out downtown!

2. Please describe the process of designing the logo "GIALOUSIS".

After an initial interview with the clients, we follow a long research procedure that helps us clearly identify all of the essential needs that we need to communicate — the things we want to show off. Then we examine the best ways to visualize the results of this research. Our early drafts and tests follow an evolutionary design procedure which ultimately leads to the final design. This was the same procedure we followed when designing the logotype for "Gialousis".

3. What is the most challenging part about logo design and how do you deal with it?

We think that the most challenging part in the design procedure of a logotype is the time we devote to the research. It's when we try to understand the project and its special needs, and usually it is also the time when the idea is born. You have a short amount of time to study — and find the best way to depict — the special needs and characteristics of a product or industry that you may not have even heard of before, or in some occasions, hasn't even existed before that project.

4. What do you perceive as the difference between logo design and other graphic design disciplines?

A logotype constitutes the base, but also the crest of a brand! As the design base, it sets the rules and defines the mood of the whole brand's visual system, and as the design crest, it secures every single application, making its presence essential.

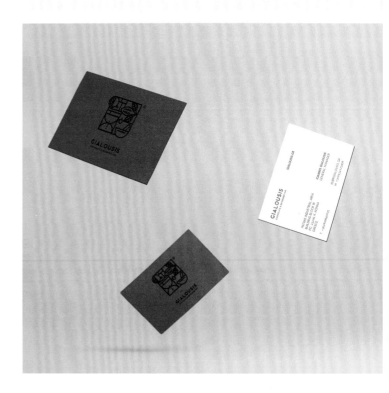

5. In your opinion what is the most important objective when designing a logo?

The most important objective when designing a logo is to create an accurate visualization of the idea that it represents. To leave the precise imprint of the brand's characteristics, whether this is immediately understood or by designing it so it inspires a "second read". It is also important for a logo to have correct functionality while also being easily recognizable.

6. More and more graphic designers are using geometric shapes to create logos. What do you think about this trend?

Choosing geometrical forms for visualizing meanings is not something new. The idea behind Greek ideograms or Egyptian hieroglyphs and other primal writing systems is the same. We can also find geometric forms with imprinted meanings in art, even in older logotypes that are known to all. Thus, when aiming for "less design" and more meaning in fewer lines, the linear approach and geometric forms might be a solution. Perhaps it characterizes the "writing" of our time, which will make it distinguishable in the future.

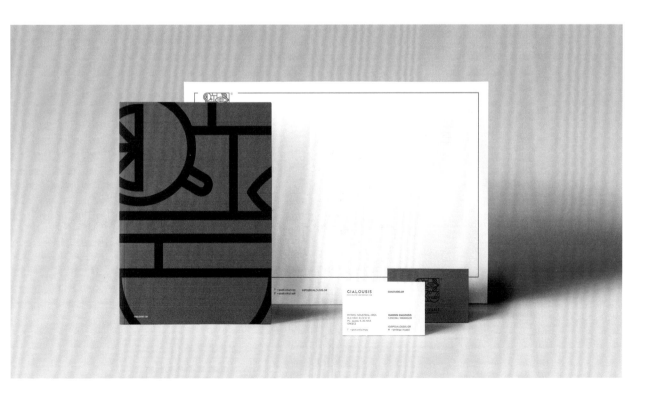

1. Passenger Pigeon X

Design: vacaliebres
Client: PPX, Mark D'Onofrio

2. Modern Pioneer

Design: The Office of Visual
Communication
Client: Modern Pioneer

3. FK Partizan

Design: Zivan Rosic
Client: FK Partizan

4. Glazed Bun

Design: Studio AIO
Client: Glazed Bun

5. Terrasa – gifs & flowers

Design: FLAT12 studio
Client: Terrasa

6. Milk & Sugar

Design: Andrea Schlaffer
Client: Milk & Sugar

1

2

3

4

5

6

7

8

7. Burger Factory

Design: Andrea Schlaffer
Client: Burger Factory

8. Sport for the World

Design: Jimbo Bernaus
Client: SFTW

9. Tokyo Olympic Games 2020

Design: Asen Petrov
Client: Japanese Olympic Committee

TOKYO
OLYMPIC
GAMES
2020

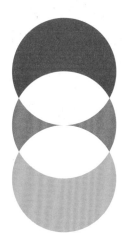

TOKYO
PARALYMPIC
GAMES
2020

9

1. Radmir Volk

Design: Radmir Volk
Client: Personal Project

2. Future Tech Team

Design: Dušan Milet
Client: FutureTech Team

3. ON THE WOK

Design: Oscar Bastidas
Client: On the Wok – Asian
Restaurant in Venezuela

4. Tygrolovy

Design: Inluw Team
Client: Tygrolovy

5. Jurydyka Garbary

Design: Fuzz Studio
Client: Jurydyka Garbary

6. Agricultural of Epidaurus

Design: POSITIVE designlab
Client: Municipality of
Epidaurus

1

2

3

4

5

6

7. FALA

Design: Abstract Logic
Client: FALA

8. Thirsty Energy

Design: Jiani Lu
Client: World Bank

9. Sweet Spoon

Design: Jimbo Bernaus
Client: Sweet Spoon
Mollerussa

10. Erasmus Barcelona Experience

Design: Jimbo Bernaus
Client: Erasmus
Barcelona Experience

11. NetCoins

Design: Esteban Oliva
Client: NerCoins –
Digital currency

12. The Campus

Design: Esteban Oliva
Client: THE Campus
– University search engine

7

8

9

10

11

12

1. To Cure Paralysis Foundation

Design: Daniel Owen Comite
Client: To Cure Paralysis Foundation

2. Proclama Profetica 2016

Design: Joshua Barillas
Client: Fjord street food

3. Diclofenac

Design: Aleksandra Godlewska
Client: Student Project

4. The Lab

Design: Andrea Schlaffer
Client: The Lab

5. Ambience

Design: Angelos Botsis
Client: Ambience, Telemarketing Services

1

2

3

4

5

**THE
LONDON
POOLS**

TIME TO GET WAVEY

6

7

6. The London Pools

Design: Jack Harvatt
Client: The London Pools

7. Marradi

Design: Jack Harvatt
Client: Marradi

8. Fjord

Design: Dock 57
Client: Fjord street food

9. Nautilus

Design: Zivan Rosic
Client: Nautilus

10. N.A.L. Financial

Design: The Office of
Visual Communication
Client: N.A.L. Financial

8

9

10

1. Capsule

Design: Jack Harvatt
Client: Capsule Studios

2. Inluw

Design: Inluw Team
Client: Inluw

3. Stoa

Design: Joshua Barillas
Client: Stoa Architects

4. MORE THAN MUD

Design: Jack Harvatt
Client: MORE THAN MUD

5. Square Pear

Design: Jack Harvatt
Client: Square Pear

6. Shimada Corporation

Design: Masaomi Fujita
Client: Shimada Corporation

1

2

3

4

5

6

7

8

7. Xchange

Design: Denys Kotliarov
Client: Xchange

8. Travel Lettering

Design: Pellisco
Client: Pellisco

9. None

Design: Morocho Estudio
Client: Personal Project

10. Campamento Internacional

Design: Joshua Barillas
Client: Campamento Internacional

11. Origolo

Design: Value Studio
Client: Origolo

9

10

11

1. Novamedia

Design: monome
Client: Novamedia

2. Madmen San Francisco

Design: Zivan Rosic
Client: Madmen San Francisco

3. Zenko Foundation

Design: Inluw Team
Client: Zenko Foundation

4. edenskin

Design: monome
Client: edenskin

5. Fox

Design: monome
Client: Fox

6. MELITEA –
honey producer

Design: POSITIVE designlab
Client: Efstratiadi Foteini

1

2

3

4

5

6

7

7. So that Explains It

Design: Bo Hao Ciou
Client: Oriental
Institute of Technology

8. Boule et Gaufre

Design: Demetris Kalambokis
Client: Boule et Gaufre
(Waffle on-the-go)

9. Dondon

Design: Kamila Figura
Client: Dondon doughnut
food truck

8

9

1. FC Skyline Yokohama

Design: Zivan Rosic
Client: FC Skyline Yokohama

2. Modern House

Design: Asen Petrov
Client: Estate Agency

3. Las Toscas

Design: Morocho Estudio
Client: Las Toscas Canning
Shopping

4. Velesstroy

Design: Abstract Logic
Client: Ivan Klimov

5. PUKI PUKI

Design: CHOCOTOY
Client: PUKI PUKI

1

2

3

4

5

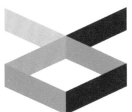

6

7

8

9

10

6. Research Square

Design: Maurizio Pagnozzi
Client: Research Square

7. Macride

Design: Maurizio Pagnozzi
Client: Maurizio Pagnozzi,
Crsistiano Vicedomini,
Denise Di Nardo

8. Chorus

Design: Bo Hao Ciou
Client: Self-initiated Project

9. Hiring Logotype

Design: Bo Hao Ciou,
Meng Chieh Li
Client: 88 Donburi

10. Every Day is a Miracle

Design: Bo Hao Ciou
Client: Self-initiated Project

1. Brick Services – 1

Design: Denys Kotliarov
Client: Brick Technology Ltd.

2. Brick Services – 2

Design: Denys Kotliarov
Client: Brick Technology Ltd.

3. Brick Services – 3

Design: Denys Kotliarov
Client: Brick Technology Ltd.

4. Brick Services – 4

Design: Denys Kotliarov
Client: Brick Technology Ltd.

5. JS Tennis Centre

Design: Denys Kotliarov
Client: JS Tennis Centre

1

2

3

4

5

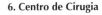

6. Centro de Cirugia

Design: sstudio™
Client: Centro de Cirugia

7. McKenzie Miller Films

Design: Odie+Partners
Client: McKenzie Miller Films

8. Birmingham Community Church

Design: Odie+Partners
Client: Birmingham
Community Church

9. Martin Plastic & Reconstructive Surgery

Design: Odie+Partners
Client: Martin Plastic &
Reconstructive Surgery

10. Endless Summer Landscapes

Design: Odie+Partners
Client: Endless Summer
Landscapes

11. After Press

Design: Odie+Partners
Client: After Press

6

7

8

9

10

11

1. EDUKOS

Design: Oscar Bastidas
Client: Edukos – Venezuelan
Restaurant in Florida

2. CREOLA

Design: Oscar Bastidas
Client: Creola – Venezuelan
Craft Beer

1

2

3. LFM. PR

Design: Dušan Miletć
Client: LFM. PR

**4. Ann Morgan,
Event Planning**

Design: Andrea Pinter

5. La Soffitta di Clodette

Design: Giada Tamborrino
Client: La Soffitta di Clodette

6. Dirty – Street wear

Design: Dawid Cmok
Client: Dirty

7. Food Surfing

Design: Cursor Design Studio
Client: Geooikonomiki SA

8. Wasted

Design: Marco Oggian
Client: Wasted

3

4

5

6

7

8

1. Sundrops Day Spa

Design: Kimmy Lee
Client: Sundrops Day Spa

2. Drake Northwave

Design: Marco Oggian
Client: Drake Northwave

3. Tower 12 Studios

Design: Nebojsa Matkovic
Client: Ruben Corona

4. Magna Carta

Design: Marco Oggian
Client: Magna Carta

5. TCS

Design: Marco Oggian
Client: TCS

6. Mamma Sferico

Design: Kevin Harald
Campean
Client: Mamma Sferico

1

2

3

4

5

6

**52
FACTORY**

7. 52 Factory

Design: Dock 57
Client: 52 Factory
creative group

8. Little, Bookshop

Design: Andrea Pinter

9. CHEKHOV

Design: Galina Khaylova
Client: CHEKHOV

10. BULLDOG'S

Design: Start Lab
Client: BULLDOG'S

11. Rentlandia

Design: Daria Stetsenko
Client: Rentlandia (Children's
goods rental store)

12. Mamgellan

Design: Nick Zotov
Client: Mamgellan

7

8

9

10

11

12

1. XPLOSIVA

Design: Marco Oggian
Client: XPLOSIVA

2. PARTNERSHIP ON

Design: EGGPLANT FACTORY
Client: ASAN NANUM FOUNDATION

3. Wood&Peak

Design: Marco Oggian
Client: Wood&Peak

4. 1LIN1 Studios

Design: Esteban Oliva
Client: 1LIN1 Studios –
Creative Video Production House

5. Kakino-Kinoshita

Design: Masaomi Fujita
Client: Kakino-Kinoshita

6. Mi Cafetal

Design: Cursor Design Studio
Client: Michos Nikolaos

1

2

3

4

5

6

KAIA

BERNOOLI

7

8

MAGDA**LOYKAKOU**
PHOTOGRAPHY

RADOSŁAW KAŹMIERCZAK
FOTOGRAFIA

9

10

PROTEU ®

GIZMOSURF
new age technology

11

12

7. Kaia Natural

Design: Nebojsa Matkovic
Client: Brabazon

8. Bernooli

Design: Steve Wolf
Client: Bernooli

**9. MAGDA LOUKAKOU
PHOTOGRAPHY STUDIO**

Design: pd-design studio
Client: Magda Loukakou
Photography Studio

10. Radosław Kaźmierczak

Design: Marta Gawin
Client: Radosław
Kazmiercźak Photography

11. Proteu

Design: Another Collective
Client: Proteu

12. Gizmosurf

Design: Anna Kuts
Client: Gizmosurf

1. Borheh

Design: Two Times Elliott
Client: Borheh

2. Saunders Bradford

Design: Odie+Partners
Client: Saunders Bradford

3. Christian Life Center

Design: Nick Zotov
Client: Christian Life Center

4. O LINE

Design: Matthieu Martigny
Client: Self-initiated Project

5. Gostest

Design: Pavel Saksin
Client: Dot Seven

6. Wychwood

Design: StudioMH
Client: Wychwood

1

2

3

4

5

6

7

8

9

10

11

12

7. Graph Paper Press

Design: Pavel Saksin
Client: Graph Paper Press

**8. Fotógrafos X
el Cambio**

Design: sstudio™
Client: Fotógrafos X
el Cambio

9. Binc

Design: Odie+Partners
Client: Binc

10. Noha Nadler

Design: Odie+Partners
Client: Noha Nadler

11. Boundary Stone

Design: Odie+Partners
Client: Boundary
Stone Financial

12. Centurion

Design: Odie+Partners
Client: Centurion
Pharmeceuticals

1. Rockvine Homes

Design: Odie+Partners
Client: Rockvine Homes

2. Royse Group

Design: Odie+Partners
Client: Royse Group

3. Clements Dean

Design: Odie+Partners
Client: Clements Dean
Building Company

4. Shelby Company

Design:Odie+Partners
Client: Shelby Company

5. Here's the Rub

Design: Odie+Partners
Client: Here's the Rub

6. Bien Fait

Design: Odie+Partners
Client: Bien Fait

1

2

3

4

5

6

7. Lammb

Design: Dave Klimek
Client: Lammb

8. The Rocket

Design: Dave Klimek
Client: The Rocket

9. Beogradski Brutalizam

Design: Zivan Rosic
Client: Beogradski Brutalizam

10. Marta Śleszyńska

Design: Marta Śleszyńska
Client: Personal project

11. Two Brilliants

Design: Nick Zotov
Client: Two Brilliants

12. C LINE

Design: Matthieu Martigny
Client: Self-initiated Project

7

8

9

10

11

12

1. Hammock

Design: Daria Stetsenko
Client: Hammock (Creative coworking space)

2. Red Sirius

Design: Fuzz Studio
Client: Red Sirius

3. Belford Garments

Design: Kimmy Lee
Client: Belford Garments

4. One

Design: Maurizio Pagnozzi
Client: One Design

5. Museum of Engineering

Design: Fuzz Studio
Client: Museum of Municipal Engineering

1

2

3

4

5

6   7

8   9

10   11

6. Book

Design: Maurizio Pagnozzi
Client: Maurizio Pagnozzi

7. Magna Carta

Design: Marco Oggian
Client: Magna Carta

8. Fedél

Design: Andrea Schlaffer
Client: Fedél

9. Artes

Design: Andrea Schlaffer
Client: Artes

10. GRUPO ENGENHO

Design: DUNA
Client: Grupo Engenho

11. Sunbreak Homes

Design: Milos Milovanovic
Client: Matt Lytle

1. Moka

Design: Giada Tamborrino
Client: Personal Project

2. Innovation box

Design: Pavel Saksin
Client: Innovation box

3. MediPLUS

Design: Kimmy Lee
Client: Self-initiated Project

4. Firestock Goods

Design: Jack Harvatt
Client: Firestock Goods

5. ALVARO CAMACHO

Design: Oscar Bastidas
Client: Alvaro Camacho –
Photographer

1

2

3

4

5

BOOKBOARD™
CONSULTING

6

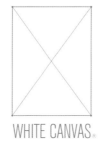

WHITE CANVAS®

7

6. Bookboard Consulting

Design: Andrea Pinter

7. White Canvas

Design: Henríquez
Lara Estudio
Client: White Canvas

8. TIOTYA MOTYA

Design: Start Lab
Client: TIOTYA MOTYA

—РЕСТОРАН—

Тётя Мотя

КУРОРТНАЯ КУХНЯ

8

1. Serendipity

Design: Asen Petrov
Client: Serendipity Jewelry Architecture

2. Fashion kids

Design: Roberto Alba
Client: Fashion kids

3. Heraf

Design: Carving Studio
Client: Heraf

4. Property Force

Design: Anna Kuts
Client: Property Force

5. La Esquina

Design: Luminous Design Group
Client: La Esquina / Bar – Restaurant

1

2

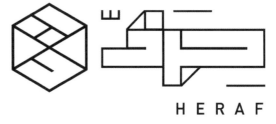

3

4

5

BATTILA™

YUM YUM
BOOKS

6

7

Tamneh School

8

9

XYLART

SINCE 1967

a r t b a r

EXPRESS YOURSELF

10

11

6. Battila

Design: Kevin
Harald Campean
Client: Battila

7. Yum Yum Books

Design: Kamila Figura
Client: Yum Yum Books

8. Tamneh School

Design: Carving Studio
Client: Tamneh School

9. Drow Ranger

Design: Dunia Mushcab
Client: Personal Project

10. Xylart

Design: Angelos Botsis
Client: Xylart Bespoke
Woodwork

11. Artbar

Design: Jiani Lu
Client: artbar

1. Bistronomie

Design: Alexander Yaguza
Client: Aleksey Skidan

2. Skinpop Studio Re Design

Design: Mostasho
Client: Skinpop Studio

3. Atelier Rennais

Design: Vivien Bertin
Client: Atelier Rennais

4. Flyover

Design: Maciej Świerczek
Client: Flyover

5. Shoshone National Forest Camp

Design: Andrea Pinter

1

SKINPOP CREATIVE STUDIO

2

ATELIER · RENNAIS
ARCHITECTURE D'INTÉRIEUR

3

4

SHOSHONE
NSFC EST 1981
NATIONAL-FOREST-CAMP
for first-time Campers
WYOMING

5

6

7

8

9

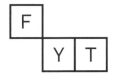

FYT JEANS
ENGINEERED
FOR COMFORT™

10

11

6. Daniel Hopwood – A

Design: Two Times Elliott
Client: Daniel Hopwood

7. Daniel Hopwood – B

Design: Two Times Elliott
Client: Daniel Hopwood

8. Koett

Design: Value Studio
Client: Koett

9. Open Architects

Design: Asen Petrov
Client: Open
Architects Keynote

10. Echo Wild Tour

Design: Asen Petrov
Client: Wild Adventure
Photography

11. FYT Jeans

Design: VOLTA Brand
Shaping Studio
Client: FYT Jeans

1. PIN MI SHI TEA SHOP

Design: Bo Hao Ciou
Client: Oriental Institute of
Technology

2. HA

Design: Matthieu Martigny
Client: Self-initiated Project

3. Blowhammer

Design: Maurizio Pagnozzi
Client: Salvatore Sinigaglia

1

2

3

4

6

7

8

9

4. EmTh Group

Design: Alexander Tsanev
Client: Hype Digital Agency

5. Geometric V

Design: Kimmy Lee
Client: Self-initiated Project

6. Filmkult

Design: Studio Goat
Client: filmkult

7. M LINE

Design: Matthieu Martigny
Client: Self-initiated Project

8. A PEOPLE

Design: Matthieu Martigny
Client: Self-initiated Project

9. A LINE

Design: Matthieu Martigny
Client: Self-initiated Project

1. Mobile Design Container

Design: Marta Gawin
Client: Design Silesia

2. DJ Marko Ross

Design: Zivan Rosic
Client: DJ Marko Ross

3. HM

Design: sstudio™
Client: Hospital Muñiz

4. Mouse

Design: Dawid Cmok

5. CusCus

Design: Margarita Petrianova
Client: Mikhail Pimenov

1

2

3

4

5

6. LABEL magazine

Design: Marta Śleszyńska
Client: Student Project

7. 8-Bit

Design: Kimmy Lee
Client: Self-initiated Project

8. SQUARE PICTURAL

Design: Matthieu Martigny
Client: Self-initiated Project

9. SQUARE POINT

Design: Matthieu Martigny
Client: Self-initiated Project

10. HIPPOPOTAMUS

Design: Matthieu Martigny
Client: Self-initiated Project

11. Vasilis Kouroupis

Design: Angelos Botsis
Client: Vasilis Kouroupis

6

7

8

9

10

11

1. G

Design: Matthieu Martigny
Client: Self-initiated Project

2. GRAPE WINE

Design: Matthieu Martigny
Client: Self-initiated Project

**3. GIAN
DOMENICO TROIANO**

Design: Kosmog
Client: GIAN DOMENICO
TROIANO

4. Teatr Śląski

Design: Marta Gawin
Client: Silesia Theatre

5. MTRL KYOTO

Design: Hiromi Maeo
(enhanced Inc.)
Client: Loftwork Inc.

6. Orion

Design: Kevin Harald
Campean
Client: Orion

1

2

3

4

5

6

7. Pickerington Crossfit

Design: Nick Zotov
Client: Pickerington Crossfit

8.Ninox

Design: Nick Zotov
Client: Ninox

9. PRISM

Design: Matthieu Martigny
Client: Self-initiated Project

10. Inside Fyi

Design: Nick Zotov
Client: Inside Fyi

11. KOSMOG

Design: Kosmog
Client: Kosmog

12. Bizzthink

Design: Creogram
Branding&Digital Agency
Client: Bizzthink

7

8

9

10

11

12

1. MICAI

Design: Hiromi Maeo
(enhanced Inc.)
Client: MICAI Limited

2. LOVE

Design: Asen Petrov
Client: Ekaterina Lachova

3. CONCEPT

Design: Asen Petrov
Client: Contemporary
Ceramic Studio

4. A2+1

Design: sstudio™
Client: A2+1 Arquitectos

5. PS86

Design: OSOM STUDIOS
Client: PS86

1

2

3

4

5

6

7

6. Opsis

Design: Angelos Botsis
Client: Opsis printing
Services

7. Românico Bordados

Design: VOLTA Brand
Shaping Studio
Client: Românico Bordados

8. OSOM CIRCLES

Design: OSOM STUDIOS
Client: OSOM STUDIOS

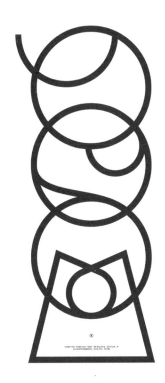

8

1. Well Business

Design: Alexander Yaguza
Client: Mikhail Fedorov

2. Creorama

Design: Creogram
Branding&Digital Agency
Client: Creogram
Branding&Digital Agency

3. Beauty Space

Design: Filipe Guimarães
Client: Beauty Space

4. OSOM CUT

Design: OSOM STUDIOS
Client: OSOM STUDIOS

consulting
Well business

CREORAMA

1

2

BEAUTY SPACE
love yourself

3

4

5

6

7

8

9

5. Funky

Design: Value Studio
(in collaboration with
First Sense)
Client: Funky

6. Archiyah

Design: Kimmy Lee
Client: Archiyah

7. True Color Studio

Design: Marco Oggian
Client: True Color Studio

8. Ishome

Design: Value Studio
Client: Ishome

9. Bloc Brands

Design: Noeeko Studio
Client: Bloc Brands

1. Beyond Aestethics

Design: Nick Zotov
Client: Beyond Aestethics

2. Life

Design: Roberto Alba
Client: Life

3. Wood Design Jewelry

Design: Stefan Grubačić
Client: Wood Design Jewelry

4. Theory & Craft

Design: Steve Wolf
Client: Theory & Craft

5. Tailgrab Clothing

Design: Marco Oggian
Client: Tailgrab Clothing

6. Ideaform

Design: Bo Hao Ciou, Meng
Chieh Li
Client: Idealform

1

2

3

4

5

6

7. GPA Construction

Design: Dunia Mushcab
Client: Melbourne Web Co.

8. Credo

Design: Pellisco
Client: Indeed

9. Music Lion

Design: Kimmy Lee
Client: Self-initiated Project

10. LEO

Design: Matthieu Martigny
Client: Self-initiated Project

11. Entre Vinhas & Mar

Design: Filipe Guimarães
Client: Entre Vinhas & Mar

12. Employ

Design: Pavel Saksin
Client: Employ

7

8

9

10

11

12

1. Cord

Design: Two Times Elliott
Client: Cord

2. Institut Psychologie

Design: Dave Klimek
Client: Institut Psychologie

3. TREE

Design: Matthieu Martigny
Client: Self-initiated Project

4. BIRD CIRCLE

Design: Matthieu Martigny
Client: Self-initiated Project

5. MOR8

Design: Oscar Bastidas
Client: Personal Brand

6. Orchard Conservatory

Design: Sean O'Connor
Client: Orchard

1

2

3

4

5

6

ENSEMBLE

In order to stand out in a competitive creative field, many logo designers create serialized variations or sets to make their logos more recognizable. The sets are based on a fundamental outline and distinguished with a variety of approaches, from distinctive patterns to multiple color schemes. Even a slight alteration on a graphic element can give a logo a completely new visual quality. This method is practical as well, with logotype variations being easy to adjust for different branding applications, such as brochures, websites, etc.

The Interview with
LAB EDUCACAO

by **Fabio Issao**

1. Where do you typically look for design inspiration?

Nature, people and systems are themes that have continually inspired me since I started drawing.

From complex organisms to indescribable landscapes, from the incorruptible set of principles that rule order and chaos of all elements to its amazing colors, shapes, scents, and behaviors, I'm always intrigued, curious and delighted when I'm close to Nature.

People are privileged containers for Knowledge and Wisdom, where Creativity, Joyfulness and Bliss are expressed in a profoundly beautiful way. From daily dialogues to transformative readings, films, and art, I invest a lot of my time getting to better know and learn with people I admire. Most of the meaningful conversations I've had throughout my career gave me the possibility of disrupting my mindset and opened my eyes to wider, brighter universes.

Systems, on the other hand, are related to the contexts, platforms, models, and types of connections that enable things to work, collaborate, prosper, and build realities in a collective dimension. I might admit this is one of my favorite issues ever, in which I'm constantly seeking to figure out what lies behind certain situations and what the drivers or reasons were that lead things to reach their current state.

2. Could you please describe the process of designing the logo "LAB Educação"?

It was quite a challenge not only to clarify their mission, vision and values, but to find a simple and clear way to translate them visually, since LAB Educação was in its initial state of development.

I started by understanding the systemic approach that permeates LAB's relationships in the education network, and, above all, the shared values that are generated among all the involved actors. Working out the connections between people and educational technologies and processes, and the transformative experiences that derive from this combination, proved to be a

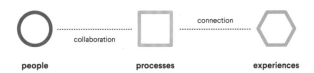

assessment

collaboration

continuous innovation

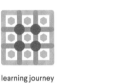

empowerment

social impact

implementation

learning journey   contextual design   user experience

frames   patterns   icons   symbols   objects

clear solution to effectively communicate LAB's essence. Finally, putting the logo's components together with a composition like that of a molecular formula added an experimental and scientific dimension which perfectly fit the meaning of LAB as "from the laboratory".

The whole branding process took around three months, with interviews and co-creative exercises to fine-tune their vision, mission, values, and brand positioning, followed by two months to develop the whole visual identity system, including the iconography, illustrations, motion graphics, and website.

3. Many of your logo works have several variations. Why do you choose these forms to present the logos?

Mostly because I believe that organizations are living organisms, which are constantly evolving, adapting, and changing along the course of their existence. Therefore, the visual assets, be it a logo or any other element, should evoke and reinforce that intrinsic dimension.

4. What do you think is the most difficult thing in designing a logo?

Bringing to light the essence of an organization, which can take a lot of time when you're trying to figure out what really distinguishes it, is definitely the hardest yet most rewarding part. When I'm able to reach that, the visual language pops out in a smooth and coherent way.

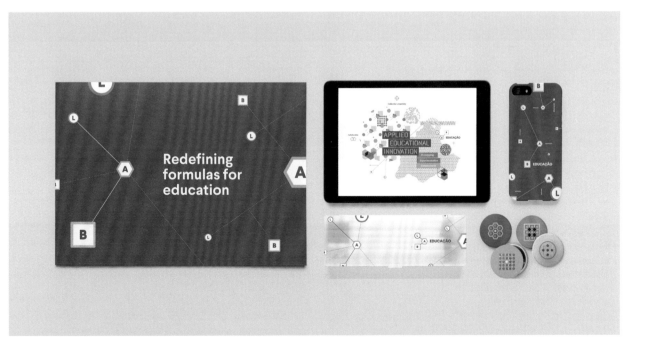

5. What do you expect trends will be in the future of logo design?

Traditional logo design is becoming more and more of a commodity, since it's conceived to be an immutable, communication-focused resource, the objective of which is to maintain control over designs as they were originally created. On the other hand, it's wholly necessary to seek ways to unleash the potential of design in order to empower what really matters: people, communication, products and services for building better, more meaningful realities.

6. What advice would you give to aspiring logo designers?

The more you're helping people to clarify their goals and refine their visions, whether by delivering visual communication or enhancing their businesses through branding methodologies, the more relevant you become for the business, enabling you to reach wider and more strategic roles that are truly about design's essence: how to solve problems and make things better.

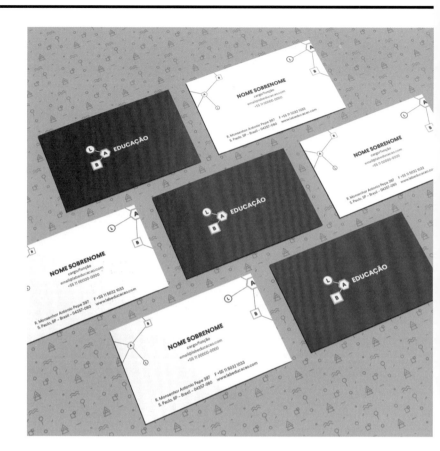

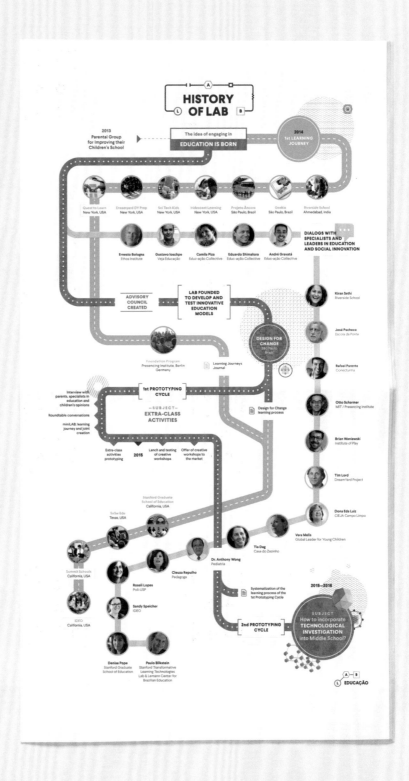

1. Vivercidade (Living Cities)

Design: Fabio Issao
Client: Vivercidade

SOCIAL EMPOWERMENT

URBAN MOBILITY

CITY EMBELISHMENTS

FOOD MOVEMENTS

URBAN GARDENING

URBAN ARTS

EDUCATION

URBAN SPORTS

CONSCIOUS SHOPPING

CITY BRANDING

1

2. Right Now Entertainment

Design: Marcelo Hoff
Client: Right Now
Entertainment

**1. Muzeum Narodowe
W Warszawie**

Design: Dawid Cmok
Client: Muzeum Narodowe
w Warszawie

MNW

↓

1. M · N · W = ⋈

2. ⋈ + ⋈ + ⋈ = ⋈

3. ⋈ → ⋈ = ⋈ → ⋈

↓

MUZEUM NARODOWE
W WARSZAWIE

MUZEUM
W NIEBOROWIE I ARKADII

MUZEUM WNĘTRZ
W OTWOCKU WIELKIM

MUZEUM PLAKATU
W WILANOWIE

MUZEUM RZEŹBY
IM. X. DUNIKOWSKIEGO
W KRÓLIKARNI

2. e-homes, Re-homes

Design: Masaomi Fujita
Client: Wood earth presents

3. CN Studio Visual

Design: Dawid Cmok
Client: CN Studio Visual

Re·HOMES e·HOMES

2

3

1. Ambasador

Design: Dawid Cmok
Client: Ambasador

2. BREA Marine Team

Design: Asen Petrov
Client: BREA Marine Team

3. EMPEROR'S BREWING

Design: Milos Milovanovic
Client: Emperors Brewing Co.

1

2

3

4. Nextshopper
Design: Maciej Świerczek
Client: Nextshopper

1. Hackademia

Design: Fabio Issao
Client: Hackademia

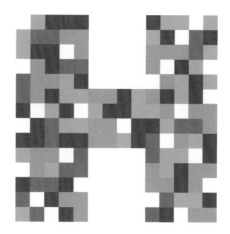

 HACKADEMIA

 HACKADEMIA
www.hackademia.com.br

     HACKADEMIA

2. Simpli.city

Design: Fabio Issao
Client: Maker Brands

3. UNUS

Design: Fabio Issao
Client: UNUS

2

3

1. Yodelity

Design: KR8 bureau
Client: Yodelity

2. 4hands

Design: Fabio Issao
Client: 4hands

1

2

3. Youngzine Fishcake

Design: EGGPLANT
FACTORY

Client: Youngzine Food

2. CHOX

Design: Aleksandra
Godlewska &
Marta Śleszyńska

Client: Student Project

3

CHOX

4

1. LPM Burgers

Design: Nebojsa Matkovic
Client: Romaric Hiem

2. FAD – Arts and Design Faculty, UNAM.

Design: Oscar EstMont
Client: Arts and Design Faculty, UNAM.

2

1. Pro Unlocks

Design: Five Designs™
Client: Pro-Unlocks

2. Armadillo

Design: Supple Studio
Client: Armadillo

1

armadillo   armadillo

armadillo   armadillo

armadillo   armadillo

2

3. Puzzle Gakuen

Design: Masaomi Fujita
Client: Puzzle Gakuen

1. 4SHORTS
Identity & Sting

Design: Supple Studio
Client: Channel 4

2. D.R.A.W.

Design: Supple Studio
Client: D.R.A.W. Recruitment

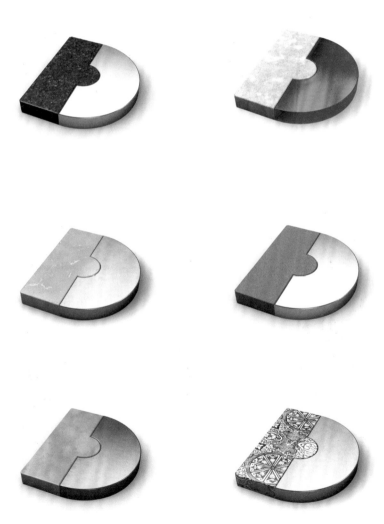

1. Diner's

Design: Alexander Yaguza
Client: Vitaliy Pejsahov

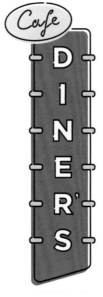

2. NONSENSE

Design: Aleksandra
Godlewska
Client: Bachelor Project

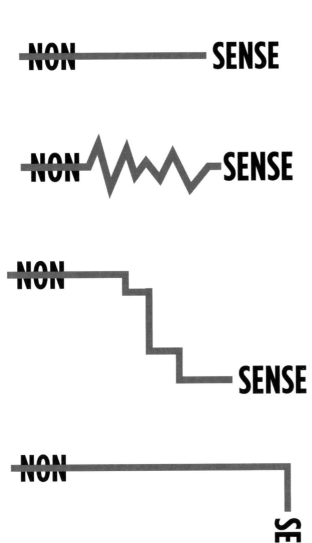

1. TECHWAVE

Design: Hiromi Maeo
(enhanced Inc.)
Client: TECHWAVE

TECHWAVE
Global

TECHWAVE
共に突き抜ける ── Break through together

TECHWAVE
Education

TECHWAVE
Content

TECHWAVE
Re:Life

TECHWAVE
Digital Health

TECHWAVE
Deploy

TECHWAVE
Re:Work

2. Le Marché Cafe

Design: Jiani Lu
Client: Le Marché Cafe

3. Ibis

Design: Zivan Rosic
Client: Ibis

2

3

1. Neus Ortiz
Design: Gerard Marin
Client: Neus Ortiz

2. Dusavon
Design: Jiani Lu
Client: Dusavon

NEUSORTIZ

INTERIORISTA

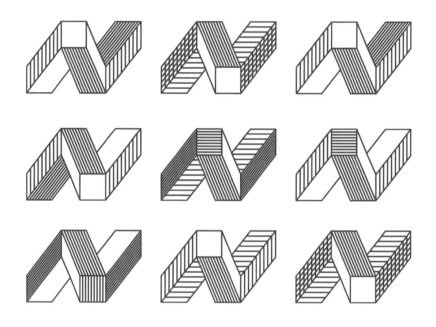

1

2

3. SKETCH NOTE
Design: Hiromi Maeo
(enhanced Inc.)
Client: Loftwork Inc.

 SKETCH NOTE

SKETCH NOTE

SKETCH NOTE   SKETCH NOTE

SKETCH NOTE   SKETCH NOTE

SKETCH NOTE   SKETCH NOTE

SKETCH NOTE   SKETCH NOTE

SKETCH NOTE   SKETCH NOTE

1. Edut

Design: Hiromi Maeo
(enhanced Inc.)
Client: Edut

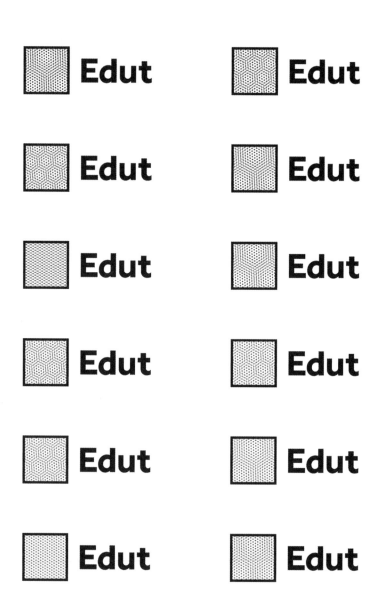

2. Habtat Coworking

Design: Marcelo Hoff
Client: Habtat Coworking

3. ITFormation

Design: Denys Kotliarov
Client: ITFormation

2

3

1. WUX3

Design: Angelos Botsis
Client: WUX3

2. Remexx

Design: Denys Kotliarov
Client: Remexx Ltd.

1

2

3. Daily Metro

Design: SSOM
Client: Self-initiated Project

M E T R O

M E T R O

⬚ E ▽ R O

metro

metro

metro

metro

metro

metro

metro

metro

metro

3

1. Janda

Design: KR8 bureau

Client: Janda Wohntraum –
Design seit 1951

2. Branding of JT Playground

Design: Kenny Ko
Client: JT Playground

3. Coinfor

Design: SSOM
Client: ITRC

4

3

1. Butcher Denim

Design: Marco Oggian
Client: Butcher Denim

2. Switchblade

Design: Marco Oggian
Client: Switchblade

3. Chocolate Box

Design: Kimmy Lee
Client: Chocolate Box, Inc.

1

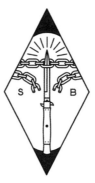 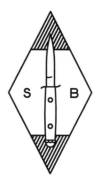

2

3

4. Honor Thy Brother

Design: Nebojsa Matkovic
Client: Honor Thy Brother

1. DUNA

Design: DUNA
Client: Estúdio Duna

2. Nozze Network

Design: Giada Tamborrino
Client: Nozze Network

3. Eva Luna

Design: Daria Stetsenko
Client: Eva Luna – Women's
sleepwear shop

4. Black Label Gift

Design: Anna Kuts
Client: Black Label Gift

2

3

4

1. NO HAY BRONCA

Design: Oscar EstMont
Client: Valentín Gurrieri

2. Leo Wine & Kitchen

Design: Alexander Yaguza
Client: Aleksey Skidan &
Sergey Podporin

1

2

3. Arts and Design
Faculty, UNAM.

Design: Oscar EstMont
Client: Arts and Design
Faculty, UNAM

FACULTAD DE
ARTES & DISEÑO
UNAM

FACULTAD DE
ARTES & DISEÑO
XOCHIMILCO

FACULTAD DE
ARTES & DISEÑO
UNAM

FACULTAD DE
ARTES & DISEÑO
XOCHIMILCO

FACULTAD DE
ARTES & DISEÑO
ACADEMIA DE SAN CARLOS

FACULTAD DE
ARTES & DISEÑO
ACADEMIA DE SAN CARLOS

FACULTAD DE
ARTES & DISEÑO
UNIDAD DE POSGRADO C.U.

FACULTAD DE
ARTES & DISEÑO
UNIDAD DE POSGRADO C.U.

FACULTAD DE
ARTES & DISEÑO
TAXCO

FAD
UNAM

FACULTAD DE
ARTES & DISEÑO
TAXCO

FAD
UNAM

1. Magadan Seafood Bar

Design: Alexander Yaguza
Client: Tipologia studio

**2. Vsegda Gotov
(Always Ready)**

Design: Alexander Yaguza
Client: Marina Lavrova

3. Riverside Coffee

Design: Alexander Yaguza
Client: Ivan Ignatov

2

3

1. EXPO 2017

Design: Marco Oggian
Client: EXPO Astana

2. Holla

Design: Anna Kuts
Client: Holla emotions

3. Kyoto Wok Cafe

Design: Alexander Yaguza
Client: Evgeniy Alekseevich

1

2

3

4. Gadget Box

Design: Pavel Saksin
Client: Gadget Box

 Gadget Box

4

1. Mesto (Place)

Design: Alexander Yaguza
Client: Maxim Myagkiy

2. Code Hipsters

Design: Alexander Yaguza
Client: Aleksey Taktarov

1

CODE H1PSTERS

CODE
H1PS
TERS

2

**3. EDIT Digital
Disruptive Education**

Design: VOLTA Brand
Shaping Studio
Client: EDIT Digital Disruptive
Education

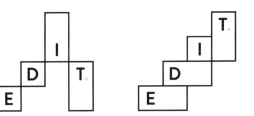

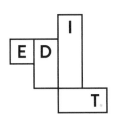
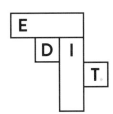
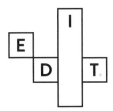

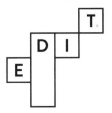
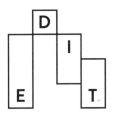
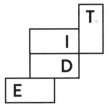

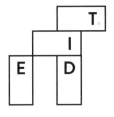
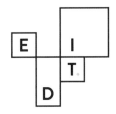
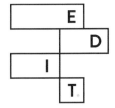

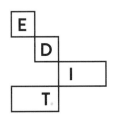
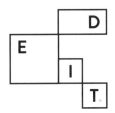
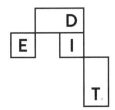

3

1. StudioMH

Design: StudioMH
Client: Personal Project

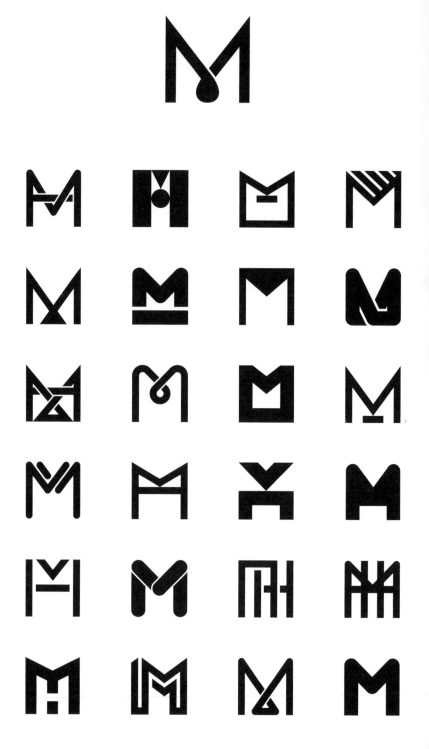

2. Magnum Wine Bar

Design: Alexander Yaguza
Client: Tipologia studio

**3. Centrum Spotkań
Kulturalnych w Lublinie**

Design: Creogram
Branding&Digital Agency
Client: Centrum Spotka
Kulturalnych w Lublinie

2

3

1. Gerard Marin

Design: Gerard Marin
Client: Gerard Marin

1

RETRO

With the development of the Internet, it has become common to see logos designed with modern techniques or digital means. However, some designers still prefer to create old-fashioned works with a sense of nostalgia. Vintage designs are always associated with the stories or spirit of a particular era; these styles not only convey familiarity and authenticity, but also highlight remarkable visual aspects of the resulting logos.

The Interview with
KITTEL'S

*by **Tobias Hall***

1. What type of information do you usually gather from the client before starting a logo?

Besides the obvious questions of what the company is or does, I usually ask the client to provide me with a list of adjectives which they feel sums the company up — not only with regards to their product but also their personality and tone of voice. I'll also ask them to provide me with style references so that I get an idea of what they're looking for stylistically.

2. Where did you begin with the logo "Kittel's"? How did you get to that essence?

I started by producing five rough sketches using the information above — these sketches were quite eclectic in style, because the client didn't have a specific style in mind. Once the client had chosen his preferred sketch, we started the development stage, in which I began to refine the logo crest and some of the smaller details — there were a lot of individual elements which needed discussing, such as which illustrations we were going to use for inside the mini roundels at the bottom of the piece. I remember there was also a lot of discussion around the style in which the peacock was drawn.

3. What is the message of the logo "Kittel's"?

Kittel's is a shop in Hamburg, Germany, which specializes in all things British. It is run by Alexander Kittel, who himself is German, but with British parents. Kittel's stocks all sorts of things, from furniture to food, but everything has a British influence.

4. How do you choose the right color and font for each logo design project? Do you have any favorite or most used fonts that you use in your projects? Why?

Brand colors will be defined by the feeling the client wants to communicate through their branding. In this case, the client had a certain color which he knew he wanted to feature in the logo, so it was up to me to incorporate it and choose other colors that would not only complement his choice but also reflect what the brand stood for. When it comes to fonts, I don't use them for the logotype itself, which is almost always entirely bespoke, but I often choose supporting brand fonts as part of the process. Again, it's about making choices which will complement the main logotype while reflecting the brand values and also delivering on practical requirements, such as legibility.

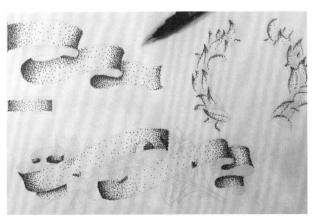

5. What is the most challenging part about logo design and how do you deal with it?

For me, the beginning of the process is always the most challenging – it's narrowing down exactly what it is the client wants to communicate through the logo. Clients aren't always the best at expressing this, and occasionally, if you are working directly for the client (as opposed to through an agency), it's easy for the client to become too "close" to the project; overly precious or anxious about their ideas and unwilling to listen to yours.

6. What do you consider the most important thing when designing a logo?

Again, for me it's about communicating the brand with one symbol. Often you'll need to consider how that symbol will stand out against the brand's competitors, too, making sure that it feels like part of the same market yet is different enough stand up against everything else and demand attention.

1. The Forge

Design: Studio AIO
Client: The Forge

2. Masshole & The Minions

Design: The Office of Visual
Communication
Client: Forward Technologies

3. Denimhead

Design: Dock 57
Client: Denimhead on-line
project

4. Nuit

Design: Noeeko Studio
Client: Nuit

5. Leader Card Game

Design: Studio AIO
Client: Leader Card Game

6. Coffee Bob

Design: Dock 57
Client: Coffee Bob
coffeeshop

1

2

3

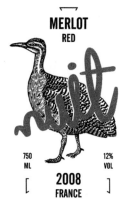

4

5

6

7

8

7. Brine Brothers

Design: Ceren Burcu Türkan
Client: Brine Brothers

8. My Angel Cafe

Design: Value Studio
Client: My Angel Cafe

9. Visual

Design: ThinkBoldStudio!™
Client: Visual Barber shop

10. Pivnushka

Design: FLAT12 studio
Client: Pivnushka

11. Shoe Maniac

Design: Dock 57
Client: Shoe Maniac
on-line project

12. Rest:public

Design: Roman Dzivulskiy
Client: Rest:public

9

10

11

12

1. Alterist Nutrients
Design: Steve Wolf
Client: Alterist Nutrients

2. Mount Gay Origin of Craft Crest
Design: Tobias Hall
Client: Mount Gay

3. Winterwell Roundel
Design: Tobias Hall
Client: Winterwell

4. Lehome Vintage
Design: Steve Wolf
Client: Lehome Vintage

5. Handy Supply Co.
Design: Steve Wolf
Client: Handy Supply Co.

6. Un Metro Adelantado
Design: Morocho Estudio
Client: Un Metro Adelantado

1

2

3

4

5

6

7

8

9

10

11

12

7. Andrew Jackson State Park

Design: Daniel Owen Comite
Client: South Carolina State Parks

8. Muzzle Loaders

Design: Milos Milovanovic
Client: Jeff Clemens

9. Bleeding Heart Brewery

Design: Kreatank
Client: Zack Lanphier

10. Bull River Charters

Design: Daniel Owen Comite
Client: Bull River Marina

11. Gatorland

Design: Daniel Owen Comite
Client: Gatorland Orlando

12. Fish Restaurant

Design: Alaa Tameem
Client: Asmak Tharaa

1. The Lace House

Design: Daniel Owen Comite
Client: The Lace House

2. Ben Vaught Crest

Design: Daniel Owen Comite
Client: Ben Vaught
Woodworker

3. Ben Vaught Woodworking

Design: Daniel Owen Comite
Client: Ben Vaught
Woodworker

4. Hambleton

Design: ThinkBoldStudio!™
Client: Hambleton

5. Brothers

Design: ThinkBoldStudio!™
Client: Brewing Brothers

6. Valhalla Pub

Design: Variant73
Client: Valhalla Pub

1

2

3

4

5

6

7

8

7. Original

Design: ThinkBoldStudio!™
Client: Original 1920

8. 69

Design: ThinkBoldStudio!™
Client: Aveiro Emotions

9. Grande Bretagne hotel

Design: POSITIVE designlab
Client: EURODOMUS S.A.

10. Louise

Design: Ceren Burcu Türkan
Client: Louise
Patisserie & Boulangerie

11. Royal

Design: ThinkBoldStudio!™
Client: The Royal barber shop

12. Zymology

Design: ThinkBoldStudio!™
Client: Zymology

9

10

11

12

1. Circe's Grotto Muse

Design: Daniel Owen Comite
Client: Circe's Grotto

2. South Carolina Crest

Design: Daniel Owen Comite
Client: South Carolina

3. BARAKA

Design: Abstract Logic
Client: BARAKA

4. Circe's Grotto Paninis

Design: Daniel Owen Comite
Client: Circe's Grotto

5. Punta Este

Design: Tobias Hall
Client: Punta Este / Estrella
de Levante

1

2

3

4

5

6

7

8

9

10

6. Phoenix Botanica

Design: Ceren Burcu Türkan
Client: Phoenix Botanica

7. Outer Shores Expeditions

Design: Milos Milovanovic
Client: Outer Shores –
Russell Markel

8. DB

Design: Abstract Logic
Client: Vadim Budnikov

9.SoapFormula

Design: FLAT12 studio
Client: SoapFormula

10. Thousand Oaks

Design: Ceren Burcu Türkan
Client: Thousand Oaks
Brewing Company

1. The Sandeman Chiado

Design: VOLTA Branding
Shaping Studio

Client: Sandeman

2. CHEESEBERRY

Design: Panfilov & Yushko
Creative Group

Client: CHEESEBERRY

3. SNG Sangue na Guelra

Design: Filipe Guimarães

Client: SNG Sangue na
Guelra

4. Prestige

Design: Panfilov & Yushko
Creative Group

Client: Prestige

5. VIA LATTA

Design: Panfilov & Yushko
Creative Group

Client: VIA LATTA

6. California Beach City

Design: Kreatank

Client: Laura Oe

1

2

3

4

5

6

7

8

9

10

11

7. Branchline Restaurant

Design: Sean O'Connor
Client: Branch Line

8. Ravouna 1906

Design: Noeeko Studio
Client: Ravouna 1906

9. Ginger

Design: ThinkBoldStudio!™
Client: Ginger Bakery

10. Casas Burnay

Design: ThinkBoldStudio!™
Client: Ana Burnay

11. Lebensecht

Design: Ceren Burcu Türkan
Client: Lebensecht

1. Brodaty Roman

Design: Dawid Cmok
Client: Brodaty Roman

2. Dan & Dave Crest

Design: Tobias Hall
Client: Dan & Dave Playing
Card Co.

3. Dan & Dave
Ace of Spades

Design: Tobias Hall
Client: Dan & Dave Playing
Card Co.

4. Khan the Conqueror

Design: Milos Milovanovic
Client: Personal Project

2

- Made in the U.S.A -

3

KHAN
THE CONQUEROR

4

1. Simonson Lumber

Design: Milos Milovanovic
Client: Peter D. Simonson

2. Caravel Brewing Co.

Design: Milos Milovanovic
Client: Claire Waters

3. Captain's Daughter

Design: Milos Milovanovic
Client: Josh Hill

4. Ponoi River (Fly fishing)

Design: Milos Milovanovic
Client: Steve Estela

5. Team Uproar

Design: Dunia Mushcab
Client: Local Good Games
store owner

6. Tobias Hall Crest

Design: Tobias Hall
Client: Self-initiated Project

1

2

3

4

5

6

7

8

9

10

11

12

7. Mad Sons Pub

Design: Milos Milovanovic
Client: Kirk Hassen

8. Mc Arthur Ranch

Design: Milos Milovanovic
Client: Justin Smith

9. Bared Footwear

Design: Milos Milovanovic
Client: Anna Baird

10. Anzac Biscuits

Design: Milos Milovanovic
Client: Russel Bradley

11. Tommy's Guns

Design: Milos Milovanovic
Client: Tommy Richards

12. Partners In Crime

Design: Steve Wolf
Client: Partners In Crime

1. Fototandem

Design: Typemate
Client: married couple of photographers

2. LAFANT

Design: Oscar Bastidas
Client: Lafant – Bohemian Female Clothing Brand

3. TAINO

Design: Oscar Bastidas
Client: Taino Aqua Ferme – Tilapia's Farm in Haiti and California

4. XVOROST

Design: Radmir Volk
Client: Xvorost workshop

5. St. Laurent

Design: Sean O'Connor
Client: Kendall Pavan

6. Fat Free

Design: Henríquez Lara Estudio
Client: Fat Free

1

2

3

4

5

6

DA THESAVRIS
MMXV
WORKING WORLDWIDE
BASED IN VARSOVIA

7

COCINA DEL MERCADO

EST 014

ALARíZ®

MAR Y TIERRA DEL
LITORAL CANTÁBRICO

8

9

· NY US ·

LA CATRINA

FLOWER STUDIO

— ✱ —

10

11

12

7. Da Thesavris

Design: Konrad Sybilski
Client: Self-initiated Project

8. Alariz

Design: Henríquez
Lara Estudio
Client: Alariz

9. Original Tusovka

Design: Inluw Team
Client: Original Tusovka

10. La Catrina

Design: Henríquez
Lara Estudio
Client: La Catrina

11. Siete Cincuenta

Design: Henríquez
Lara Estudio

Client: Siete Cincuenta

12. Embaixador

Design: Filipe Guimarães
Client: Embaixador

1. Oregon camp

Design: Dock 57
Client: Oregon Camp clothing brand

2. Hobo and Sailor

Design: Dock 57
Client: Hobo and Sailor clothing brand

3. Manzo

Design: Studio AIO
Client: Manzo

4. Black Fox Press

Design: Dock 57
Client: Black Fox Press

5. Mr. Frankenstein's Brainsicles

Design: Dunia Mushcab
Client: Personal Project

6. Melbourne Web Co.

Design: Dunia Mushcab
Client: Melbourne Web Co.

1

2

3

4

5

6

7

8

9

10

11

12

7. Lucerne, Zirben Schnaps

Design: Andrea Pinter

8. Aboard, Original Boat Wear

Design: Andrea Pinter

9. Royal Honey

Design: Andrea Pinter

10. Glenfield, Rabbitry and Farm

Design: Andrea Pinter

11. Bird Wood

Design: Typemate
Client: Wood workshop in Cheliabinsk

12. Tyaga bar

Design: Typemate
Client: Hookah bar in Moscow / Logomachine

1. Black Magic

Design: Mostasho
Client: Black Magic Music,
Clothing, Tattoo shop

2. Noot

Design: Alexander Shimanov
Client: Noot

**3. The Organic Cotton
Candy Company**

Design: The Office of Visual
Communication
Client: Touchpoint Marketing

4. Skinpop Studio Emblem

Design: Mostasho
Client: Skinpop Studio

5. Versus

Design: Mostasho
Client: Gurú Gallery

1

2

3

4

5

THE CONNOISSEUR

WHISKY COLLECTION

6

DGO   MED

7

8

LOUCOMOTION

IMAGERY LAB & APPS FACTORY

Since 2014

9

10

11

6. The Connoisseur

Design: Ceren Burcu Türkan
Client: The Whisky Collection

7. Tres Quince Emblem

Design: Mostasho
Client: Restaurant 315 /
Nadia Ontiveros

8. KUTI

Design: Mostasho
Client: Vladimir VelGut / KUTI
Company

9. Loucomotion

Design: Milos Milovanovic
Client: Caetano Brasil

10. Mill City Fineries

Design: Milos Milovanovic
Client: Matt Brunnette

11. SALAMI & CO.

Design: Oscar Bastidas
Client: Salami & Co. – Coffee
Shop and Bakery
in United Kingdom

**1. Scissor & Co. –
The Barber Shop in Genoa**

Design: vacaliebres
Client: Scissor & Co.

2. Marco Gadau

Design: vacaliebres
Client: Marco Gadau

3. Darek Novak

Design: vacaliebres
Client: Darek Novak

4. In Motus Veritas

Design: vacaliebres
Client: In Motus Veritas

**5. Wolfpack
Striders RFNO.1**

Design: Daniel Owen Comite
Client: Wolfpack Striders

6. Tres Quince Logotype

Design: Mostasho
Client: Restaurant 315 /
Nadia Ontiveros

1

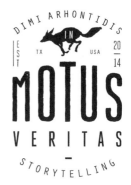

2

3

4

5

6

7

8

9

10

11

7. The Hake

Design: Nebojsa Matkovic
Client: The Hake

8. CFG Barbell Club

Design: Nebojsa Matkovic
Client: CFG Barbell Club

9. Fantasma

Design: Nebojsa Matkovic
Client: Fantasma Clothing

10. Granville Wines

Design: Nebojsa Matkovic
Client: Granville Wines

11. Hamburgueria Alfaiate

Design: Filipe Guimarães
Client: Hamburgueria Alfaiate

1. Supreme F.C.

Design: Roberto Alba
Client: Supreme F.C.

2. Fresh Cutz

Design: Andrea Schlaffer
Client: Fresh Cutz

3. Ushuaia

Design: Roberto Alba
Client: Ushuaia

4. Maria

Design: Marta Gawin
Client: Polish Chemistry

5. House warming Invitation

Design: Dunia Mushcab
Client: Personal Project

6. Snackeriet

Design: ThinkBoldStudio!™
Client: Tamara Kuklina

1

2

3

4

5

6

7. Vegetar. Blog

Design: Filipe Guimarães
Client: Inês Furtado

8. Encontro Comtradição

Design: Filipe Guimarães
Client: Comtradição

9. Produbov

Design: Alexander Shimanov
Client: Produbov

10. Sail away with me

Design: Alexander Shimanov
Client: Flaster

11. Free Callisthenics

Design: Value Studio
Client: Free Callisthenics

12. Kokovin's Film

Design: Value Studio
Client: Kokovin's Film

7

8

9

10

11

12

1. MAGA VII

Design: Filipe Guimarães
Client: Maga Mostra de Artes Visuais

2. Hortosintra

Design: Filipe Guimarães
Client: Hortosintra

3. Risk Everything Crest

Design: Tobias Hall
Client: Self-initiated Project

4. Modernjak

Design: Milos Milovanovic
Client: Brian Garcia

1

2

3

4

5. Mercado Lincoln

Design: Misael Osorio
Client: Mercado Lincoln

6. Eulogio

Design: Henríquez
Lara Estudio
Client: Eulogio

7. Noble Farmer

Design: Milos Milovanovic
Client: Rob Dinn

MERCADO

5

6

7

1. Toreador – Butcher

Design: Dawid Cmok
Client: Toreador

2. Viomio

Design: Alexander Yaguza
Client: Peter Karasev

1

2

INDEX

A

Abstract Logic
www.behance.net/Abstract_Logic
Pages 015, 023, 066, 126, 129, 134, 142, 157, 191, 198, 292, 293

Alaa Tameem
www.alaatameem.com
Pages 018, 039, 042, 052, 055, 069, 098, 134, 135, 158, 289

Aleksandra Godlewska
www.behance.net/agodlewska
Pages 131, 192, 247, 255

Alexander Morgan
www.linkedin.com/in/arcmorgan
Pages 015, 020, 026, 068, 126, 131, 149

Alexander Shimanov
www.behance.net/shimanov
Pages 081, 089, 102, 115, 304, 309

Alexander Tsanev
www.behance.net/tsanev
Pages 014, 017, 020, 023, 073, 122-125, 126, 129, 221

Alexander Yaguza
www.behance.net/rayinbruges
Pages 092, 096, 106, 218, 228, 254, 270, 272, 273, 274, 276, 279

Andrea Pinter
www.behance.net/andreapinter
Pages 014, 021, 116, 139, 142, 156, 171, 203, 205, 215, 218, 303

Andrea Schlaffer
www.behance.net/andrea_schlaffer
Pages 016, 027, 090, 113, 147, 148, 188, 189, 192, 213, 308

Angelos Botsis
www.angelosbotsis.com
Pages 024, 032, 033, 044, 048, 071, 075, 095, 096, 097, 106, 116, 182, 192, 217, 223, 227, 262

Anna Kuts
www.behance.net/anna_kuts
Pages 028, 030, 031, 034, 041, 042, 043, 044, 049, 056, 156, 158, 159, 166, 167, 170, 173, 207, 216, 269, 274

Another Collective
www.anothercollective.pt
Pages 058-061, 093, 109, 112, 113, 117, 160, 162, 165, 178, 179, 207

Asen Petrov
www.asenpetrov.com
Pages 024, 025, 040, 050, 051, 075, 092, 189, 198, 216, 219, 226, 242

B

Bo Hao Ciou
www.behance.net/cioubohao
Pages 078, 079, 118, 119, 152, 184, 197, 199, 220, 230

Botond Vörös
www.botondvoros.com
Pages 024, 051, 054, 146, 180, 182

C

Carving Studio
www.carvingjo.com
Pages 129, 143, 166, 174, 175, 216, 217

Ceren Burcu Türkan
www.behance.net/cerenburcuturkan
Pages 287, 291, 293, 295, 305

CHOCOTOY
www.behance.net/chocotoy
Pages 149, 198

Chris Trivizas
www.christrivizas.gr
Pages 026, 154, 155, 172, 183

Creogram Branding &Digital Agency
www.creogram.pl
Pages 103, 106, 114, 176, 183, 225, 228, 279

Cursor Design Studio
www.cursor.gr
Pages 107, 153, 160, 162, 183, 203, 206

D

Daniel Bodea Kreatank
Pages 164

Daniel Owen Comite
www.danocomite.com
Pages 021, 022, 023, 150, 180, 182, 192, 289, 290, 292, 306

Daria Stetsenko
www.behance.net/dariastetsenko
Pages 032, 035, 038, 153, 164, 182, 205, 212, 269

Dave Klimek
www.daveklimek.eu
Pages 030, 031, 046, 052, 053, 055, 089, 092, 211, 232

Dawid Cmok
www.behance.net/dawidcmok
Pages 028, 041, 080, 089, 093, 104, 126, 128, 137, 147, 163, 181, 203, 222, 240, 241, 242, 296, 312

Demetris Kalambokis
www.behance.net/Demetris_K
Pages 094, 104, 111, 133, 139, 169, 170, 197

Denys Kotliarov
www.kotliarov.com
Pages 017, 019, 021, 022, 074, 075, 195, 200, 261, 262

Dock 57
Sveta Shubina, Manar Shajri
www.behance.net/dock_57
Pages 120, 142, 143, 149, 174, 175, 193, 205, 286, 287, 302

DUNA
Raimundo Britto
www.behance.net/raimundobritto
Pages 016, 071, 105, 213, 268

Dunia Mushcab
www.behance.net/duniamushcab
Pages 097, 114, 172, 217, 231, 298, 302, 308

Dušan Miletć
www.behance.net/Wardz
Pages 018, 019, 071, 074, 075, 099, 190, 203

E

EGGPLANT FACTORY
Bobae Kim, Youngji Jung, Jeyoun Lee
www.eggplantfactory.co.kr
Pages 206, 247

Esteban Oliva
www.estebanoliva.com
Pages 068, 144, 146, 147, 191, 206

F

Fabio Issao
www.fabioissao.com
Pages 234-237, 238, 244, 245, 246

Filipe Guimarães
www.behance.net/piua
Pages 056, 080, 177, 228, 231, 294, 301, 307, 309, 310

Five Designs™
www.behance.net/fivecreativity
Pages 040, 250

FLAT12 studio
Yana Klochihina
www.flat12.ru
Pages 021, 112, 132, 133, 134, 135, 146, 188, 287, 293

Fuzz Studio
Paweł Hahn, Nikola Hahn
www.fuzzstudio.pl
Pages 021, 023, 066, 071, 099, 105, 110, 126, 142, 190, 212

G

Galina Khaylova
Pages 205

Gerard Marin
www.gerardmarin.com
Pages 258, 280

316

Giada Tamborrino
www.giadaland.com
Pages 027, 035, 047, 089, 093, 107, 116, 161, 164, 170, 203, 214, 269

H

Henríquez Lara Estudio
www.henriquezlara.com
Pages 027, 034, 040, 047, 168, 171, 172, 215, 300, 301, 311

Hiromi Maeo (enhanced Inc.)
www.behance.net/enhanced_hiromimaeo
Pages 076, 224, 226, 256, 259, 260

I

Inluw Team
Serhiy Fedynyak, Alexander Derega
www.behance.net/serhiyFE
www.behance.net/derega
Pages 023, 062, 132, 148, 190, 194, 196, 301

Insando
www.behance.net/Insando
Pages 082, 083, 183

J

Jack Harvatt
www.behance.net/JackHarvatt
Pages 070, 073, 150, 151, 193, 194, 214

Jiani Lu
www.lujiani.com
Pages 077, 191, 217, 257, 258

Jimbo Bernaus
www.behance.net/jimbobernaus
Pages 062, 064, 065, 087, 189, 191

Joshua Barillas
www.behance.net/joshuabarillas
Pages 076, 115, 144, 178, 181, 192, 194, 195

John Soultanidls
Pages 139

K

Kamila Figura
www.behance.net/kamilafigura
Pages 134, 138, 147, 161, 169, 197, 217

Kenny Ko
www.kooooo.hk
Page 265

Kevin Harald Campean
www.behance.net/HaraldKevin
Pages 040, 094, 105, 107, 184, 204, 217, 224

Kimmy Lee
www.behance.net/KimmyLee
Pages 026, 027, 035, 043, 044, 055, 086, 087, 098, 101, 105, 108, 109, 110, 111, 113, 114, 156, 160, 161, 166, 172, 173, 204, 212, 214, 221, 223, 229, 231, 266

kissmiklos
www.kissmiklos.com
Pages 067, 099, 111, 156, 162, 168

Konrad Sybilski
www.konradsybilski.com
Pages 051, 068, 076, 113, 167, 169, 175, 177, 301

Kosmog
Alessio Pompadura
www.behance.net/Kosmog
Pages 106, 224, 225

KR8 bureau
www.kr8bureau.at
Pages 050, 077, 097, 246, 264

Kreatank
Daniel Bodea
www.kreatank.com
Pages 127, 129, 135, 164, 165, 289, 294

L

Luminous Design Group
www.luminous.gr
Pages 042, 130, 138, 156, 161, 167, 169, 171, 179, 185-187, 216

M

Maciej Świerczek
www.maciejswierczek.pl
Pages 051, 072, 086, 127, 137, 157, 218, 243

Marcelo Hoff
www.behance.net/marcelohoff
Pages 239, 261

Marco Oggian
www.mrcggn.com
Pages 157, 167, 203, 204, 206, 213, 229, 230, 266, 274

Margarita Petrianova
www.behance.net/Atira
Pages 048, 222

Marta Gawin
www.martagawin.com
Pages 090, 099, 109, 112, 162, 163, 177, 178, 184, 207, 222, 224, 308

Marta Śleszyńska
www.behance.net/martasleszynska
Pages 133, 211, 223

Masaomi Fujita
http://tegusu.com
Pages 079, 146, 148, 194, 206, 241, 251

Matteo Orilio
www.behance.net/MatteoOrilio
Page 162

Matthieu Martigny
www.behance.net/matthieumartigny
Pages 047, 049, 050, 051, 052, 053, 054, 055, 208, 211, 220, 221, 223, 224, 225, 231, 232

Maurizio Pagnozzi
www.mauriziopagnozzi.com
Pages 010-013, 026, 042, 142, 199, 212, 213, 220

Meng Chieh Li
Pages 078, 119, 152, 184

Milos Milovanovic
www.behance.net/Milos_Milovanovic
Pages 044, 213, 242, 289, 293, 296, 298, 299, 305, 310, 311

Misael Osorio
www.dribbble.com/misa9
Pages 014, 016, 017, 020, 034, 044, 127, 131, 133, 311

monome
Julien Perraudin
www.monome.net
Pages 018, 019, 196

Morocho Estudio
www.morochoestudio.com
Pages 016, 072, 090, 148, 195, 198, 288

Mostasho
www.facebook.com/mostasho
Pages 029, 047, 048, 218, 304, 305, 306

N

Nebojsa Matkovic
www.behance.net/NebojsaMatkovic
Pages 044, 106, 114, 177, 180, 204, 207, 248, 267, 307

Nick Zotov
www.behance.net/nick_zotov
Pages 039, 047, 051, 054, 097, 205, 208, 211, 225, 230

Noeeko Studio
www.noeeko.com
Pages 054, 068, 069, 082, 096, 098, 153, 168, 173, 175, 229, 286, 295

O

Odie+Partners
www.odiepartners.com
Pages 025, 028, 029, 033, 038, 039, 041, 046, 047, 048, 049, 201, 208, 209, 210

Oscar Bastidas
www.mor8graphic.com
Pages 022, 023, 071, 083, 157, 181, 190, 202, 214, 232, 300, 305

Oscar EstMont
www.behance.net/OscarEstMont
Pages 249, 270, 271

OSOM STUDIOS
Mr Walczuk
www.mr-osom.com
Pages 046, 169, 181, 226, 227, 228`

P

Panfilov & Yushko Creative Group
Dmitry Panfilov
www.py-group.ru
Pages 032, 080, 102, 131, 179, 184, 294

Pavel Saksin
www.behance.net/paul_saksin
Pages 040, 043, 046, 049, 100, 104, 208, 209, 214,
231, 275

pd-design studio
Panagiotis Doukas
www.pdstudio.gr
Pages 068, 112, 127, 138, 142, 149, 174, 207

Pellisco
John Freddy Antolinez Rodriguez
www.behance.net/pellisco
Pages 195, 231

POSITIVE designlab
John Soultanidis
www.positive.net.gr
Pages 022, 127, 139, 140, 148, 190, 196, 291

R

Radmir Volk
www.behance.net/radmirvolk
Pages 140, 160, 171, 190, 300

Roberto Alba
www.behance.net/robert_ab
Pages 100, 104, 114, 216, 230, 308

Roman Dzivulskiy
www.behance.net/dzroman
Pages 063, 064, 066, 067, 069, 140, 182, 287

S

Sean O'Connor
www.behance.net/sean_oconnor
Pages 036, 104, 110, 111, 158, 159, 161, 167, 173,
232, 295, 300

SSOM
Minji Kim, Seongeun Lee, Sumin Lee
www.kim-minji.com
Pages 263, 265

sstudio™
Santiago Balán
www.sstudio.com.ar
Pages 038, 039, 049, 050, 097, 099, 103, 120, 201,
209, 222, 226

Start Lab
Galina Khaylova
www.start-lab.ru
Pages 172, 182, 205, 215

Stefan Grubačić
www.behance.net/stefangrubacic
Pages 015, 041, 042, 043, 135, 138, 143, 149,
165, 230

Steve Wolf
www.stevewolf.co
Pages 072, 093, 130, 146, 164, 177, 207, 230,
288, 299

Studio AIO
Moodhi Alghanim, Ahmed Alrefaie
www.studioaio.com
Pages 066, 069, 072, 096, 110, 111, 116, 128, 129,
132, 133, 136, 137, 140, 143, 146, 147, 148, 149,
170, 179, 188, 286, 302

Studio Goat
www.studiogoat.com
Pages 090, 091, 093, 120, 163, 221

StudioMH
Mike Harrison
www.studiomh.co.uk
Pages 025, 053, 102, 208, 278

Supple Studio
www.supplestudio.com
Pages 250, 252, 253

T

The Office of Visual Communication
www.theofficeofvc.com
Pages 130, 131, 136, 188, 193, 286, 304

ThinkBoldStudio!™
Hugo Marques
www.thinkboldstudio.com
Pages 287, 290, 291, 295, 308

Tobias Hall
www.tobias-hall.co.uk
Pages 086, 102, 282-285, 288, 292, 296, 298, 310

Two Times Elliott
www.2xElliott.co.uk
Pages 033, 050, 052, 053, 054, 055, 092, 208, 219, 232

Typemate
Vova Egoshin
www.typemate.pro
Pages 034, 036, 063, 084, 085, 091, 103, 107, 110, 117, 140, 161, 170, 300, 303

V

vacaliebres
Alberto Vacca Lepri
www.vacaliebres.com
Pages 036, 037, 100, 133, 156, 171, 184, 188, 306

Value Studio
www.valuestudio.net
Pages 038, 064, 077, 095, 103, 117, 145, 178, 179, 180, 195, 219, 229, 287, 309

Variant73
Adilson Porto Junior
www.variant73.com
Pages 074, 080, 139, 158, 290

Vivien Bertin
www.vivienbertin.com
Pages 083, 169, 218

Vlad Penev
www.vladpenev.com
Pages 035, 042

Vladislav Smolkin
www.smolkinvladislav.com
Pages 073, 154, 155, 157, 165

VOLTA Branding Shaping Studio
www.volta.pt
Pages 075, 095, 103, 145, 219, 227, 277, 294

W

Wiktor Ares
www.behance.net/WiktorAres
Pages 070, 088, 173

Z

Zahidul Islam
www.99designs.com/profiles/336415
Pages 067, 128, 135, 137, 181

Zivan Rosic
www.zivanrosic.com
Pages 018, 019, 033, 145, 166, 176, 188, 193, 196, 198, 211, 222, 257

ACKNOWLEDGEMENTS

We would like to thank all of the designers involved for granting us permission to publish their works, as well as all of the photographers who have generously allowed us to use their images. We are also very grateful to many other people whose names do not appear in the credits but who made specific contributions and provided support. Without these people, we would not have been able to share these beautiful works with readers around the world. Our editorial team includes editor Hannah Fu and book designer Dingding Huo, to whom we are truly grateful.